Fearless Investing Series: Mutual Funds Workbook ❶ ❷ ❸

Maximize Your Fund Returns

Published by John Wiley & Sons, Inc., Hoboken, New Jersey.
Published simultaneously in Canada.

For general information about our other products and services, please contact our Customer
Care Department within the United States at 800-762-2974, outside the United States at
317-572-3993 or fax 317-572-4002.

Wiley also publishes its books in a variety of electronic formats. Some content that appears in
print may not be available in electronic books. For more information about Wiley products,
visit our Web site at www.wiley.com.

ISBN: 0-471-71187-X

Printed in the United States of America
10 9 8 7 6 5 4 3 2 1

Introduction

In the 1990s, it seemed that anyone could pick a strong-performing mutual fund and assemble a winning portfolio. With the tailwind of a buoyant market helping them, even relatively poor funds were able to score robust gains.

The past five years, however, have proved far more challenging for investors. Following a brutal bear market from 2000 through early 2003, the industry became engulfed in scandal, dogged by allegations of improper trading and unscrupulous sales practices.

Amid that backdrop, however, investors' faith in mutual funds as a fundamentally sound investment vehicle hasn't been shaken. Investors sent nearly $400 billion to mutual funds in 2003 and 2004. In so doing, they acknowledged that funds, with their built-in diversification and professional management, remain the best way for individuals to build long-term wealth.

We at Morningstar certainly believe that to be true. The year 2004 marked our company's 20th anniversary of providing investors with the information they need to make sound financial decisions. Along the way, we've talked to scores of investors who, empowered by Morningstar's objective research and analysis, have used mutual funds to achieve goals big and small: sending kids to college, remodeling houses, and enjoying worry-free retirements.

Helping even more investors reach their goals was the impetus behind Morningstar's new Fearless Investing Series. The series, as its name suggests, is designed to demystify the often-complex world of investing—and even make it fun. In addition to grounding you, the investor, in the basics of mutual funds, our interactive workbook series gives you concrete advice for selecting the best funds for you and putting the pieces together into a portfolio that delivers maximum long-term returns.

Although the books are sold individually, the three workbooks in the series are designed to be used in conjunction with one another. Book One, *Find the Right Mutual Funds*, provides an overview of how mutual funds work, as well as a discussion of how to evaluate a fund's manager, portfolio, risk/return potential, costs, and tax efficiency. Book Two, *Diversify Your Fund Portfolio*, discusses the keys to building a diversified, all-weather portfolio and gives you concrete pointers for selecting both bond and international funds. The series culminates with Book Three, *Maximize Your Fund Returns*. In this book, you'll find advanced strategies for maximizing your portfolio's return, along with our best tips for bear-proofing your portfolio and knowing when to sell.

Within each workbook, you'll find that we've divided each lesson into four distinct sections: the lesson itself, Fearless Facts, a quiz, and a worksheet. Each workbook also includes an Investing Terms section, a list of additional Morningstar resources, and a Recommended Reading section. Read on for details about how to get the most out of each section.

Lessons: The lessons are designed to give you an overview of a particular topic, along with plenty of real-life examples and concrete tips for putting the knowledge to work in your portfolio.

Fearless Facts: These scannable lists provide you with a quick overview of the key points from the lesson. Use our Fearless Facts to brush up on what you've just learned.

Quizzes: The quizzes help ensure that you've mastered the key concepts in the lesson. You'll find answers for each of the quizzes at the back of each book.

Worksheets: The worksheets are designed to help you put the key concepts in each lesson into practice. You'll find that many of the worksheets ask you to find facts about your own funds and portfolio; the goal of these exercises is to help you understand what you own and to ensure that your portfolio suits your goals and risk tolerance.

Investing Terms: Although Morningstar's Fearless Investing Series assumes that readers do not have any background in finance or investments and thus explains any term mentioned in the text, you can look to the Investing Terms section for a more in-depth definition of each term used in the series.

Additional Morningstar Resources: Morningstar's Fearless Investing Series is designed as an introduction to Morningstar's approach to selecting mutual funds and building portfolios. Investors interested in learning more about Morningstar's other products should consult this list.

Recommended Reading: This is a list of some of Morningstar's favorite books about mutual funds and investing.

Whether you're a novice investor or a seasoned hand looking to maximize your portfolio, we trust that you'll find Morningstar's Fearless Investing Series to be a practical and profitable way to learn about mutual funds and meet your financial goals. We wish you luck on your journey.

Acknowledgments

A number of individuals played a significant role in the production of the Fearless Investing Series. Susan Dziubinski, Peter Di Teresa, and David Harrell, developed most of the lessons that form the basis of the three books in the series. Scott Berry, Christopher Traulsen, Andrew Gogerty, Russel Kinnel, Kunal Kapoor, and Joseph Nasr also contributed valuable content. Morningstar's copy-editing staff, including Elizabeth Bushman and Jason Stipp, worked hard to ensure that the concepts in the book would be clear to novice investors.

Alla Spivak and Erica Moor shepherded the books through the publishing process, coordinating the work of all of the contributors. Morningstar's design staff, notably Lisa Lindsay, Minwha Kim, David Silva, and David Williams, developed the books' design. David Pugh, our editor at John Wiley & Sons, gave us valuable guidance for completing this book.

We also owe a huge debt of gratitude to Catherine Odelbo for helping develop the series' concept. As head of Morningstar's retail business unit, she has been central to putting Morningstar's motto of "Investors First" into action.

Finally, we're grateful to Morningstar founder Joe Mansueto, who founded this company on the principle that all investors are entitled to high-quality independent investment information. His company has grown by leaps and bounds since Joe founded it 20 years ago, but Morningstar has never deviated from that central principle.

Contents

continued

continued...

Getting the Most from Your Growing Portfolio

Lesson 301: Shades of Value

Everyone has a different definition of value. For example, you and your best friend are comparing footwear (or grocery stores, plumbing services, or even housing). You call your shoes a deal because you got them on sale—50% off! Your friend, meanwhile, considers her shoes a value buy simply because she paid less than she would have for a comparable brand.

Fund managers who buy value stocks express similar differences of opinion. All value managers buy stocks that they believe are worth significantly more than the current share price, but they tend to argue about just what makes a stock a good deal. How a manager defines value will determine what his or her portfolio includes and, ultimately, how the fund performs.

Why Shading Matters

Consider the following as a great example of why investors need to understand how their fund managers define value. Clipper and Pimco PEA Value are both large-cap funds that fall into the value side of the Morningstar style box, but their performances over the past few years have been startlingly different. In 2002, for example, Pimco PEA Value lost 24.8%, while Clipper slid a mere 5.5%, ending the year in the top percentile of the large-value set.

More recently, though, Pimco PEA Value has turned in top-rung performances (a 44.4% gain in 2003 and a 6% gain for the year to date through October 20, 2004), while Clipper has had a rougher go of it, gaining just 19% in 2003 and heading into the red thus far in 2004.

What made the difference? Different definitions of value and different investment time horizons. Pimco PEA Value manager John Schneider tends to look at value by examining price ratios, such as price/earnings and price/sales, and tries to identify companies he believes can deliver positive surprises to drive those valuations higher in the future. He has a short investment horizon, with the fund's annual turnover rate hovering between 150% and 200% for most of his tenure at the fund. In 2002, Schneider found a number of beaten-up technology stocks that met his criteria. But the catalysts he saw weren't recognized by the market until much later, and the fund paid a heavy price. In 2003, however, the technology bet paid off in a big way, leading the fund to its great showing.

Clipper, meanwhile, also emphasizes cheap stocks, but its managers want to invest in dominant franchises that are out of favor but have the makings of good long-term holdings. Indeed, the fund's annual turnover is much lower than Pimco PEA Value's—typically in the 25% to 60% range. Clipper's managers also have a stricter definition of value—they look for dominant franchises that are trading at a discount of 30% or greater to their intrinsic worth. The managers estimate this using discounted cash-flow analysis or the prices of comparable companies. They're also willing to sit on outsized cash stakes when opportunities are scarce—in other words, if they don't see something they like, they won't play in the market. Technology stocks are rarely cheap enough for them to consider, and they don't typically invest in companies based on near-term opportunities. As a result, the fund is less vulnerable to the sort of risk that hurt Pimco PEA Value in 2002, but it is also less likely to participate in the turn-around of recovering sectors: In 2003, for example, the portfolio missed the rallying hardware and software stocks that lifted returns for its competitors.

Value strategies roughly divide into the relative-value and absolute-value camps. Not surprisingly, there are a lot of variations within each group.

Relative Value

Fund managers practicing relative-value strategies compare a stock's price ratios (such as price/earnings, price/book, or price/sales) with a benchmark and then make a decision about the firm's prospects. In other words, value is relative. These benchmarks can include one or more of the following:

The Stock's Historical Price Ratios. Companies selling for lower ratios than usual can be attractive buys for value managers. Often, these companies' prices are lower due to some "bad news," to which the market often overreacts. Some value managers picked up beleaguered Martha Stewart Living Omnimedia after it fell sharply, suspecting that the founder's legal troubles might be shorter-lived than expected.

The Company's Industry or Subsector. A manager may believe that a company is undeservedly cheap compared with its competitors. For example, when cell-phone handset giant Nokia was hurt by an earnings miss in 2003, the managers of Lazard Equity bought it because it looked cheap relative to other technology stocks. Funds that look for companies that are cheap relative to their industry peers may well take on more price risk than absolute-value funds. For example, in early 2000, even though the technology sector as a whole was dramatically overvalued, a relative-value manager might have continued buying technology stocks that appeared cheap relative to other technology stocks.

The Market. In this case, managers look for companies that appear attractively valued relative to the broader equity market, not just their industry peer groups. For such a manager, technology stocks wouldn't have been a likely place to find bargains in early 2000, even though many would have filled the bill for a manager seeking companies that were merely cheap relative to their industry peers. For these managers, a company may be attractively valued because of issues specific to its own operations that have depressed its share price or because it's in an out-of-favor industry. This scenario is common with cyclical sectors, such as industrials. Investors have fled consumer-services industries in 2004, for example, but managers at Oakmark Fund have quietly increased their positions in H&R Block and the Gap.

Absolute Value

Managers such as Legg Mason Value's Bill Miller and the team at Longleaf Partners follow absolute-value strategies. They don't compare a stock's price ratios with something else. Rather, they try to figure out what a company is worth in absolute terms, and they want to pay less than that figure for the stock.

Absolute-value managers determine a company's worth using a variety of factors, including the company's assets, balance sheet, and likely future earnings or cash flows. They may also study what private buyers have paid for similar companies.

Price matters

One quick way to find out just what kind of value manager you've chosen is to look at the average price multiples of the portfolio. (These are available in shareholder reports, of course, and they're also available in Fund Reports on Morningstar.com.) You'll want to know whether the fund is buying more expensive or less expensive stocks than other offerings in the category.

Holding appreciating stocks isn't necessarily bad. It could mean the manager is letting the portfolio's winners ride. As stocks appreciate to fair value, they're no longer "value" picks and your portfolio could be shouldering some increased price risk.

While Legg Mason Value and Longleaf Partners have owned some of the same companies, such as Hughes Electronics in 2002, each takes a slightly different approach to absolute-value investing—which leads to different results.

When examining a company's growth prospects, Legg Mason's Miller is more forward-looking, and often more optimistic, than many of his peers. Thus, you'll find more high-growth stocks, such as online retailer Amazon.com, in this fund than you would in the portfolios of other absolute-value managers—including that of Longleaf Partners, which doesn't hold a single software or hardware stock (as of June 2004). That difference has mattered quite a bit recently. In 2003, a year in which the market favored technology stocks, Legg Mason Value beat Longleaf Partners by nearly 10 percentage points. Thus far in 2004, however, the situation has reversed, and Longleaf has fared significantly better in a tough market than Legg Mason Value has.

Legg Mason Value

Portfolio Analysis 03-31-04

Share change since 03-04 Total Stocks:33	Sector	PE	YTD Ret%	% Assets
Nextel Communications	Media	10.59	-4.53	7.65
Tyco International	Ind Mtrls	31.48	23.70	6.85
Amazon.com	Consumer	54.42	-31.74	6.70
UnitedHealth Group	Health	22.15	29.88	5.71
⊕ InterActiveCorp	Consumer	55.50	-26.29	5.11
MGIC Investment	Financial	12.77	12.13	3.52
Bank One	Financial	—	—	3.37
Washington Mutual	Financial	11.91	1.96	3.36
J.P Morgan Chase & Co.	Financial	16.75	9.52	3.30
⊖ Waste Management	Business	21.26	-1.12	3.29
⊕ AES	Utilities	35.81	17.58	3.07
Electronic Arts	Software	25.29	0.23	3.04
Eastman Kodak	Goods	29.13	22.47	2.95
Citigroup	Financial	14.95	-3.44	2.91
⊕ eBay	Consumer	103.39	53.61	2.83
⊕ McKesson	Health	12.24	-13.87	2.75
⊕ Qwest Communications Int	Media	—	-21.06	2.65
Albertson's	Consumer	21.31	6.87	2.49
Home Depot	Consumer	19.62	16.88	2.44
WPP Grp	Business	—	—	2.43

Longleaf Partners

Portfolio Analysis 06-30-04

Share change since 03-04 Total Stocks:22	Sector	PE	YTD Ret%	% Assets
Walt Disney	Media	22.9	7.03	5.35
FedEx	Business	26.3	33.37	5.22
Aon	Financial	9.8	-8.14	4.74
Vivendi Universal	Media	—	—	4.54
NIPPONKOA Insurance	Financial	—	—	4.52
⊕ General Motors	Goods	7.1	-26.29	4.29
Yum Brands	Consumer	19.1	27.17	4.18
⊕ Comcast	Media	—	—	4.01
Hilton Hotels	Consumer	35.6	14.70	3.83
The Directv Group	Media	—	1.03	3.58
Waste Management	Business	20.3	-5.80	3.54
Philips Elec(Kon)	Goods	—	—	3.54
⊖ Pioneer Natural Resource	Energy	10.2	2.56	3.45
Level 3 Communications	Telecom	—	-41.40	3.27
Telephone and Data Syste	Telecom	32.6	17.47	2.91
Diageo	Goods	—	—	2.58
TrizecHahn	Financial	—	—	2.46
Knight Ridder	Media	17.9	-9.56	2.43
Vivendi Universal ADR	Media	—	10.42	1.31
⊖ Marriott International A	Consumer	24.5	17.89	1.26

Source: Morningstar Mutual Funds

When Value Managers Sell

There are two chief reasons value managers will sell a stock: It stops being a value, or they realize that they made a bad stock pick.

Stocks stop being good values when they become what managers call fairly valued. That means that the stock is no longer cheap by whatever value measure the manager uses. For relative-value managers, that could mean that the stock has gained so much that its price ratios are now in line with industry norms. For an absolute-value manager, that could mean that the stock's price now reflects the absolute worth the manager has placed on the company.

A manager may also sell a stock because it looks less promising than it did initially. In particular, new developments may lead the manager to a less favorable evaluation of the company. Nevertheless, if the stock's price drops but the manager believes the company itself is still attractive, that may be a chance to buy even more of it.

Fearless Facts

▶ Learn to love a sale. The value column of the Morningstar style box is one place in which some funds put up strong relative returns while enjoying limited volatility.

▶ Know your style. Relative-value managers look for stocks selling cheaply relative to the fund's historic performance, the broad industry, or the general market. Absolute-value managers research the company thoroughly, assess its worth, and only buy if the company's share price is below that figure.

▶ Do some independent research. By now you know that you can read shareholder reports for an explanation of your fund manager's approach. However, most reports won't use terms such as "relative" and "absolute." If you're interested in getting a sense of the style your manager is using, eyeball the fund's sector weightings. If the fund is focused on typically cheap sectors such as financials, energy, or industrial materials, there's a good chance it's an absolute-value fund. If it owns a number of stocks from "growth" sectors such as technology or health care, it's more likely to be a relative-value fund.

11

Quiz

1   All value managers:

Answers to this quiz can be found on page 271

   a   Buy stocks that they believe are worth significantly more than the current price.

   b   Buy stocks whose price/earnings ratios are below the market's price/earnings ratio.

   c   Buy stocks whose price/book ratios are below their historical levels.

2   Relative-value managers:

   a   Buy stocks that are cheaper than the company's entire worth.

   b   Buy stocks trading below their historical price ratios, their industry peers, or the market.

   c   Seek high growth.

3   Absolute-value managers:

   a   Buy stocks that are cheaper than what they deem to be the company's entire worth.

   b   Buy stocks trading below their historical price ratios, their industry peers, or the market.

   c   Seek high growth.

4   Which statement is true?

   a   All absolute-value managers calculate a company's worth the same way.

   b   All relative-value managers compare a stock's price/book ratio with the price/book ratio of similar stocks.

   c   Value managers fall into the relative or absolute styles, but their styles can still differ significantly within those camps.

13

continued...

5   If a stock is fairly valued, what does that mean?

a	The stock is no longer cheap by whatever benchmark the manager uses.
b	The stock has gained so much that its price/book ratio is now in line with that of its industry.
c	The stock's price currently reflects the absolute worth the manager has estimated for the company.

Worksheet

Examine your portfolio. Do you own any funds that have the word "value" in their names? Are their managers using relative-value or absolute-value approaches? How can you tell?

If you own any value funds, look at their Morningstar reports on Morningstar.com. Have your funds tended to perform better than the S&P 500 Index when the market has been down? If so, why do you think that might be?

Compare the portfolios of two funds that use value-oriented investing strategies, such as Legg Mason Value and Longleaf Partners. How are they similar? How are they different? How have their performance patterns differed?

If you invest in individual stocks, do you follow a value-oriented stock-picking strategy? Why or why not?

Lesson 302: Shades of Growth

Not everyone loves a sale. After all, sales can be messy and tiring and you can pick up some real duds along the way, whether it's a sale on shoes or refrigerators or an old house that has dry rot underneath the hardwood floors.

Value and growth are often considered opposites in investing, and for good reason. Most growth managers are more interested in a company's earnings or revenues and a stock's potential for price appreciation than they are in finding a bargain. Thus, growth funds will usually have much higher average price/earnings and price/book ratios than value funds, as the managers are willing to pay more for a company's future prospects. Value managers want to buy stocks that are cheap relative to the company's current worth or some other benchmark.

Of course, growth managers have different styles, just like value managers do. And not surprisingly, those styles have a big effect on how a fund performs and how risky it is.

Earnings-Driven

The majority of growth managers are earnings-driven, which means they use a company's earnings as their yardstick for growth. If a company isn't growing significantly faster than the market average or its industry peers, these managers aren't interested.

Within this earnings-driven bunch, momentum managers are by far the most daring. Momentum investors buy a rapidly growing company that they believe will deliver a quarterly earnings surprise or other favorable news that will drive the stock's price higher. Managers who follow this style try to buy a stock just prior to a positive earnings announcement (that is, when a company announces that its earnings are higher than Wall Street analysts predicted) and sell it before it misses an estimate (that is, when its earnings fall below what analysts thought they would be) or has other negative news. Momentum managers pay little heed to stock prices. Their funds, therefore, can feature ultra-high price multiples. They also tend to have high annual turnover rates, which can make for big capital-gains payouts and poor tax efficiency. One of the best-known proponents of this style is Garrett Van Wagoner, manager of Van Wagoner Emerging Growth, a volatile fund.

Some managers seek earnings growth in a different way. Instead of searching for stocks with the potential to surprise during earnings season, these managers seek stocks that boast high yearly growth rates: generally between 15% and 25%. But like momentum investors, managers who employ this strategy typically ignore stock prices, so their funds' price multiples can be sky-high. This investment style also encourages high portfolio-turnover rates. MFS Emerging Growth follows this kind of strategy, buying stocks with 25% and higher projected earnings growth and often featuring very high price multiples. Thus, although this strategy is different in principle from momentum investing, the results are often similar.

The most moderate earnings-growth-oriented managers look for stocks growing in a slow but steady fashion. The slow-and-steady group usually buys blue-chip stocks such as Wal-Mart and Gillette. As long as these stocks continue to post decent earnings, slow-and-steady managers tend to hold on to them. Steady-growth funds often have more modest price ratios than their peers. But when reliable growers take the lead, these funds endure as much price risk as the more aggressive funds. Funds known for following this moderate-earnings-growth strategy include American Funds Growth Fund of America and Fidelity Blue Chip Growth.

The growth field is varied and there's often a pretty big spread between the category's luxury shoppers and players that buy more moderately priced stocks. If you want to know just where your growth fund shakes out, it's often best to look at a portfolio's average P/E ratio. Check to see whether your fund is buying more expensive stocks than other players in the group.

You'll note that some of the category's biggest players are going after appreciating stocks. This performance chasing is part of their strategy. After all, they're momentum investors: As share prices rise, they climb aboard.

Price matters here too

Revenue Driven

Of course, not all growth companies have earnings. In particular, younger companies may be unprofitable for years until their businesses reach critical mass. Some growth managers will buy companies without earnings if the companies generate strong revenues. (Revenues are simply a company's sales; earnings are profits after costs are covered.)

Because there is no guarantee that firms without earnings will ever turn a profit, this approach can be risky.

Growth at a Reasonable Price

Managers who seek growth at a reasonable price (GARP) try to strike a balance between strong earnings and good value. Some managers in this group find moderately priced growth stocks by buying the rejects of momentum investors; often, these stocks have reported disappointing earnings or other bad news. GARP managers also look for companies that have been ignored or overlooked by market analysts and that are therefore still selling cheaply. Like value investors, GARP investors try to find companies that are only temporarily down and out and that have some sort of catalyst for growth in the works.

Because many GARP managers are sensitive to high price tags, this group of growth funds often features lower-than-average price multiples than the flat-out growth funds we discussed in the preceeding section. As a result, these funds can land in the blend column of the Morningstar style box. GARP funds also tend to have lower turnover rates than pure-growth funds and are therefore generally more tax-efficient than more aggressive growth offerings. Prominent GARP funds include T. Rowe Price Growth Stock and Gabelli Growth.

Mixing It Up

Few managers stick to just one kind of growth strategy. Instead, most blend a variety of stock-picking approaches. AIM Weingarten, for example, buys both core stocks—companies that grow slowly and reliably—and faster-paced momentum names. Fidelity Large Cap Stock primarily invests in GARP-type stocks, but in the past it has owned names without earnings, such as the fledgling biotech concern Cephalon. Thanks to this diversity, these funds can perform better than their narrower peers across a wider variety of market environments.

Fearless Facts

▶ When it comes to growth investing, it's vital to know the lingo.

▶ What's the difference between earnings and revenue? When managers talk about earnings, they are usually referring to the net income for a company during a given period—the amount of profit a company realizes after all costs, expenses, and taxes have been paid. When they talk about revenues, they're referring to how much the company might have earned before it subtracted business, depreciation, interest, and tax costs.

▶ One prominent subset of growth managers uses a GARP (growth-at-a-reasonable-price) approach. Think of GARP as a hybrid of the value and growth strategies.

Quiz

1 A manager following an earnings-momentum style would be most likely to sell which stock?

Answers to this quiz can be found on page 271

> a The stock of a company that has just announced strong quarterly earnings.
>
> b The stock of a company that has announced it will merge with another company.
>
> c The stock of a company that has reported lower-than-expected quarterly earnings.

2 Moderate-growth stocks such as Wal-Mart are likely to be found in which type of growth fund?

> a A fund that buys stocks featuring steady and consistent annual growth rates.
>
> b A fund that is willing to buy stocks that don't have earnings.
>
> c A value-oriented fund.

3 GARP stands for:

> a Growth and revenue pressure.
>
> b Growth with annual rates in excess of price.
>
> c Growth at a reasonable price.

4 Which one of the following funds is likely classified as a blend fund according to Morningstar?

> a A fund that follows a GARP style.
>
> b A fund whose stocks have an average annual growth rate of 20%.
>
> c A fund that buys momentum stocks.

continued...

5 Momentum strategies typically produce funds with:

a	High portfolio turnover and low risk.
b	High portfolio turnover and high risk.
c	Low portfolio turnover and good tax efficiency.

Worksheet

Do you own any funds with "growth" in their names? Based on what you've read, can you tell what types of strategies your growth managers employ? GARP? Earnings momentum? Or some other type of growth strategy?

Look at the Morningstar Fund Reports on Morningstar.com for a few of the growth funds in your portfolio. What are their average P/E ratios? Are their P/E ratios higher than that of the average for their categories? What about their long-term earnings-growth rates?

Many growth funds performed quite well in the late 1990s, when tech stocks paced the market. Did your fund perform well, on an absolute basis and relative to its peers, during those years? How did it perform during the bear market from 2000 through 2002?

Lesson 303: Using Focused Funds

Focused funds (also known as concentrated, compact, select, or nondiversified funds) have become very popular in the past few years. Many fund families now offer at least one.

Should you buy one? And if so, what should you look for? Before answering those questions, let's examine what exactly we mean when we talk about focused funds.

What Are They?

There is no standard definition for focused funds. The most common reference point is the number of individual stocks a fund holds. Generally, a focused fund will hold fewer than 40 stocks, and some of the most focused funds, such as Oakmark Select, hold just 20 names. Find how many stocks a fund holds by checking its portfolio in its shareholder report or looking at the Portfolio section of its Morningstar Fund Report.

Numbers aren't everything: A fund can also be considered focused if it concentrates a large percentage of its assets in its top 5 or 10 holdings. (This style is a common byproduct of investment strategies that also limit the fund's number of holdings to fewer than 40 stocks.) Columbia Acorn Select, for example, is considered a focused fund; it devoted nearly one-fourth of its assets to its five largest holdings in 2004.

Finally, focused can refer to a diversified fund's sector exposure. Some funds concentrate in only one or a few market sectors. For example, CGM Focus invests in just a few industries, favoring telecom, consumer services, and industrial materials in 2004. Sometimes, but not always, funds can become focused by sector because they own few individual stocks.

Why Would You Want One?

Buying a fund with a limited number of holdings is similar to picking a bunch of individual stocks—except that you don't pick those stocks yourself. Focused-fund managers often run these portfolios in addition to managing more diversified funds. Their focused funds are those in which they invest heavily in their favorite stocks or "best ideas," without worrying much about diversification or risk control. These managers usually argue that they're better able to generate superior returns by closely following a handful of top-quality stocks rather than a large collection of names.

A few great stocks can indeed have a big effect on a compact portfolio's returns. Van Kampen Global Franchise had a solid year in 2003, thanks in part to its position in tobacco stocks. Similarly, a single issue or a few troubled stocks can drag a focused fund down. Just look at Alliance Premier Growth. Its large positions in scandal-tainted stocks including Tyco, Tenet Healthcare, and, most notably, Enron proved poisonous to the fund's 2002 returns: The fund lost 33% that year. In 2004, the fund is being hurt by a miserable performance from top-five pick Intel. In contrast, one bad apple isn't likely to ruin the returns of an index fund or other fund with hundreds of holdings.

Given the added risk of investing in a focused fund, consider your own tolerance for short-term volatility. Would you be comfortable owning a fund that loses several percentage points in a matter of days? Could you stomach owning a fund that severely underperforms its category for a year or more? Even risk-tolerant investors will probably only want to buy a focused fund for a well-diversified portfolio and relegate it to their portfolio's most aggressive spot. Concentrated funds can be particularly useful counterweights to S&P 500 index funds or other broadly diversified funds.

What to Look For

If you think your investment portfolio could use a focused fund, look for the following five qualities before you buy.

When it comes to focused funds, the captain matters—a lot. At many focused funds, managers are often given free rein when it comes to investing styles and strategies, so portfolios can change quickly, trading costs can escalate, and you can find your large-blend holding becoming a small-growth vehicle (or vice versa) in a fairly short time. That's fine if you know and trust your manager, but this is one area in which a lot of research and a little caution can pay off in spades.	**Managers matter**

Experienced management. Because so much rides on the individual stocks in a focused fund's portfolio, it is crucial that you look for a fund run by a seasoned manager. Few fund managers cut their teeth on a focused fund. Usually, they get their start in the industry running fairly well-diversified portfolios. Look at the performance and risk records of the funds the manager has run in the past. Did those funds produce better performance than their category peers? It's even better if a manager already has a long and solid record running a focused fund.

Investing with Experienced Managers

Category	Manager Experience	Turnover (%)	5-Yr Return (%)
Large Blend	Most	65.67	5.58
	Least	96.55	3.20
Large Value	Most	57.07	20.08
	Least	74.52	12.74
Large Growth	Most	110.69	-9.46
	Least	81.39	-13.56
Small Blend	Most	91.24	93.80
	Least	95.58	73.74

Data through March 31, 2004

We compared the most experienced and least experienced quartiles of the above categories from 1998 and measured how they behaved over the next five years.

A reputable fund family. In conjunction with an experienced manager, look for focused funds from proven fund families. Some firms are better known for their stock-picking ability than others, and families that offer extensive research capabilities are probably a good bet. Also, look for a fund from a family known for its quality control. Does the family tolerate long periods of underperformance? Or does it take action, as Vanguard does with its subadvised funds when it sees something it doesn't like? (A fund is subadvised when the company offering the fund hires outside managers to run it. Vanguard does that with many of its non-index equity funds.) Families with reputations to protect are likely to be more vigilant than recent startups that have nothing to lose.

Strong long-term performance. You may be attracted to a focused fund because of a great quarter or sensational year. But because focused funds are linked so tightly to a few stocks or sectors, most of them will have a few glory days. Instead, look for a fund that has done well over time. If managerial experience at a previous fund is not available, then make sure the fund you're interested in buying possesses at least a solid three-year record.

Modest expenses. As with any other fund purchase, check the cost before you write your check. You should avoid any focused fund with an expense ratio higher than 2%.

Risk-busting approach. Most focused funds are risky investments by their very nature, but even in this arena there are ways you can reduce risk. Consider a fund that follows a value strategy, rather than a growth strategy. Clipper is a value-oriented focused fund. You might also consider a fund that's focused in its number of holdings but that has some sector diversification, making it less vulnerable to economic cycles.

Fearless Facts

▶ Remember, any fund with fewer than 40 stocks is probably taking on some significant company-specific risk. It may not call itself a focused fund, but it's behaving like one.

▶ Know what kind of focus you own. Does the fund hold just a few stocks? Does it run a fairly large portfolio, but devote an outsized portion of assets to its top-5 or top-10 picks? Or does it hold many stocks from just one industry?

▶ Stay on top of your focused fund. Check the portfolio to see whether or not the manager's bets, or commitments to one or two companies, have ballooned since you bought the fund.

▶ Figure out how much you're willing to risk. Focused funds can take a dive when an individual stock suffers; think of the plummeting share prices of Enron and Tyco when the news of their financial mismanagement hit the press. If you're not willing to smile through a rough ride, a focused fund might not be for you.

Quiz

1   Which of the following would not qualify as a focused fund?

Answers to this quiz can be found on page 272

a	A fund that owns 35 individual stocks.
b	A fund that has the exclusive attention of its manager.
c	A fund that invests 70% of its assets in its top-10 holdings.

2   In terms of risks and rewards, investing in a focused fund is similar to investing in:

a	An index fund.
b	A fixed-income fund.
c	A basket of individual stocks.

3   Which of the following should you expect when you invest in a focused fund?

a	Occasional short-term volatility.
b	An inexperienced manager.
c	High expenses.

4   Which is the biggest benefit of buying a focused fund from an established and reputable fund family?

a	Established fund families usually have the best managers.
b	Their funds are usually less expensive.
c	They will probably intervene if the fund underperforms over a long period of time.

continued...

5   Which focused fund should you be wary of?

   a   A fund with 30 or 40 stocks.

   b   A fund that concentrates in a few sectors.

   c   A fund with a 2% expense ratio.

Worksheet

What is a focused fund and what role can such a fund play in your investment portfolio?

Why are focused funds so much more risky than other mutual funds? On the flip side, what do concentrated funds have to offer that other funds do not?

If you are already invested in a focused fund, what did you look for when making your decision to invest? Does your focused fund court any risks beyond concentration, such as price risk or sector concentration?

Why is evaluating the quality of management so important when picking a focused fund?

Lesson 304: Style-Box-Specific vs. Flexible Funds

Legendary fund manager Peter Lynch would take some heat today.

The former head of Fidelity Magellan was an opportunist. Sometimes he liked growth stocks. Other times, value investments held more allure. Large companies struck his fancy but so did smaller firms. Today, financial advisors, investors, and the media criticize this kind of flexibility. They'd rather have managers who stick to one part of the Morningstar style box. In other words, they want style-specific managers.

Morningstar seems to be among the purists. After all, we categorize funds by narrow investment styles, such as large growth or small value. But we don't necessarily favor funds that stay in the same part of our style box year in and year out. In fact, while we know that style-specific funds have their charms, we acknowledge that flexible funds also have advantages. Neither one is better than the other. It's up to you to decide how to use each in your portfolio.

Flexibility's Power, Purity's Charms

Lynch isn't the only fund-industry luminary who insists on having the freedom to pursue his best ideas, wherever they may lie. Take celebrated First Eagle Global manager Jean Marie Eveillard: He wouldn't be half the manager he is if he couldn't pluck any type of security from any corner of the world. And even with U.S. funds, some of the best managers, including Excelsior Value & Restructuring star, David Williams, are drifters who refuse to tether themselves to any one section of the Morningstar style box.

But flexible funds have their downside: They can make building a portfolio tricky. After all, if a fund is a small-cap fund one day and has large-company tendencies the next, how can investors be sure they're really diversified? No wonder advisors, investors, and the media are wary of flexible funds.

Flexible—sort of	Not all flexible funds are daring opportunists. One of our favorites is behemoth Vanguard Total Stock Market Index. Of course, it's not truly flexible insofar as its manager has no say in where it invests. On the other hand, it crosses market-cap sizes and styles. It has a straightforward style, it's cheap, and it adds diversification to just about any portfolio. Not too shabby.

Style-specific funds, meanwhile, tend to cleave to one part of our style box. They always invest in, say, small-value stocks or mid-cap growth stocks. Families such as Putnam and T. Rowe Price offer funds that tend to stay put. As you can imagine, it's much easier to build and monitor a portfolio of style-pure funds. If you select four funds that invest in different ways, you can be confident that they'll continue to invest that way. Thus, you're always sure that you're diversified.

Using Flexible Funds

Writing off flexible funds altogether can mean tossing aside some great funds and fund managers. Here's how even style-specific devotees might work flexible funds into a portfolio.

Give away some but not all control. Use style-specific funds at the core of your portfolio. Treat them as building blocks to meet your asset-allocation goals and save a portion of assets for flexible funds. That way, your overall asset allocation won't get beyond your control.

Because change is a given, monitor flexible funds carefully. Keep an eye on where and why your flexible fund's manager is moving. And if you choose to devote significant assets to more than one flexible fund, enter your portfolio in Morningstar.com's Instant X-Ray to take note of how your overall portfolio is positioned. Instant X-Ray will tell you how much you have in each investment style. If all of your flexible-fund managers are favoring large-growth stocks, you may want to assume they know something you don't and let them ride. Or you may want to temper that bet somewhat. In any event, know what you own.

Fearless Facts

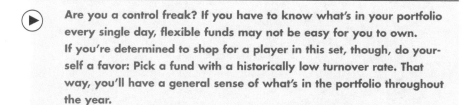 Are you a control freak? If you have to know what's in your portfolio every single day, flexible funds may not be easy for you to own. If you're determined to shop for a player in this set, though, do yourself a favor: Pick a fund with a historically low turnover rate. That way, you'll have a general sense of what's in the portfolio throughout the year.

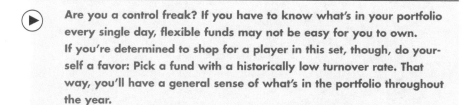 Remember, using flexible funds makes building a portfolio pretty tricky. If you favor these offerings, be sure to stay on top of your sector, country, and company exposure. You can do this using Morningstar's Instant X-ray or by examining your fund's Web site and SEC filings often.

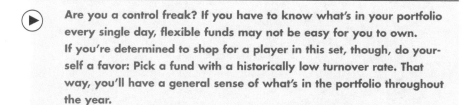 Even if you love many of the flexible funds out there, you're better off using the stick-in-the-mud style-specific offerings for your core portfolio. These funds should be your main tools to achieve your asset-allocation goals.

Quiz

1 Managers who run flexible funds:

a	Stick to one area of the Morningstar style box.
b	Invest in securities of various sizes and styles.
c	Usually work at Putnam or T. Rowe Price.

Answers to this quiz can be found on page 272

2 Flexible-fund managers:

a	Return more than style-box purists.
b	Return less than style-box purists.
c	May return more or less than style-box purists.

3 It is easiest to build and maintain:

a	An all flexible-fund portfolio.
b	An all style-box-specific-fund portfolio.
c	A mix of both.

4 If you choose to use flexible funds in your portfolio, which of the following is not a good idea?

a	Using them as core holdings and not monitoring them.
b	Monitoring them closely.
c	Using them outside your core.

5 If two of your flexible-fund managers are both favoring the same type of stocks at some point in time:

a	You should sell one of the funds to eliminate overlap.
b	You should leave the funds as is—the fund managers know something that you don't.
c	You need to decide whether you're comfortable with the imbalance.

Worksheet

What are the advantages and disadvantages of investing in a flexible
fund? What are the advantages and disadvantages of investing
in a style-specific fund?

How can you use flexible funds in your portfolio? Why is it hard to use
flexible funds as the core of your portfolio?

As is the case with focused funds, the quality of a flexible fund's
manager is extremely important to the success or failure of the fund.
How would you evaluate a flexible-fund manager before deciding
whether to invest with him or her?

Lesson 305: Sector-Fund Investing

Everyone knows you can start a fire using a magnifying glass: Grade school kids routinely put this optics lesson to the test. This experiment teaches a valuable lesson: Focus is a powerful thing.

The power of focusing is the principle behind sector funds, mutual funds that invest in a specific industry. How powerful can sector investing be? At the end of 1999, 9 of the 10 funds with the best 10-year returns were technology funds.

Such stellar returns are often the reason investors flock to particular sectors, such as technology during 1999, financials in the mid-1990s, and, more recently, to the natural resources and defense sectors in 2004. While sector investing offers great potential, it offers great risk, too. The standard deviation (the variation of a fund's monthly returns around its average monthly return) of the average technology fund is double the S&P 500's.

In this lesson, we'll discuss the variety of sector funds available, ways you might—or might not—use them in a portfolio, and what to look for when buying a sector fund.

The Many Flavors of Sector-Fund Investing

Investors have many sector funds to choose from, spanning eight different Morningstar categories: communications, financials, health-care, natural resources, precious metals, real estate, technology, and utilities.

Some sector funds focus more narrowly, homing in on a particular subsector of an industry. For example, the GenomicsFund is categorized as a health-care fund, but it invests almost exclusively in genomics or genomics-related stocks—a fairly small industry. Then there's Fidelity Select Wireless, which is a telecom fund that focuses entirely on wireless service providers and gearmakers. Given their more concentrated focus, these funds are often even more volatile than the typical sector fund.

Do You Need a Sector Fund?

Not according to John Bogle, the founder of Vanguard funds and the granddaddy of index investing, who is firm: "You could go your entire life without ever owning a sector fund and probably never miss it." But Vanguard offers sector funds such as Vanguard Health Care and Vanguard Energy. Bogle's point is simply that a well-diversified portfolio doesn't need sector funds.

Let's take an example. If you owned Vanguard Total Stock Market Index, you'd have all of the major U.S. industries covered. The fund's portfolio would range from nearly 3% in utilities stocks to about 13% healthcare issues as of March 31, 2004. Your other significant exposure would be 22% in financials and 10% in industrial materials. That's pretty broad diversification, so you might not need or want to invest additionally in a sector fund—especially not one focused on bank stocks or health-care firms, or anything else significantly represented in the index.

Using Sector Funds to Diversify

This is the bringing-coals-to-Newcastle rule: If a sector is already well represented in your portfolio, why buy more of it? If you're going to make use of a sector fund, it should add something your portfolio lacks, or it should increase your exposure to a sector that is underrepresented in your portfolio.

If you're eyeing a sector fund, now is the time to get vigilant about your existing portfolio. You need to know exactly what you own in order to find holes that could be filled with a sector offering. You can obtain sector information by looking up each of your fund's sector weightings in shareholder reports.

Sector funds take coordination

To determine whether you should buy more funds in a particular sector, you need to know and monitor your portfolio's sector weightings. Say you owned equal amounts of Vanguard 500 Index and Vanguard Growth Index in August 2004, for example. Approximately 17.6% of your portfolio is health-care stocks, but just 1.3% is devoted to utilities. More conservative investors who like the dividends that utilities stocks often pay out might want to right that imbalance with a utilities sector fund.

Speculating with Sector Funds

It can be so tempting to dive into a part of the market that you think will soar based on some trend, an analyst's recommendation, or your gut. Morningstar isn't a fan of this kind of speculation, but if you must, do it sensibly. Reserve a very small slice of your portfolio—say 5% or less—for such activities and make sure the remainder of your portfolio is well-diversified and designed to meet your long-term investment goals with a level of risk that is acceptable to you. Finally, understand that when you speculate, you may be wrong—in other words, be prepared to lose that 5% of your portfolio.

We also recommend that you avoid buying a fund that's already hot. Investors who fall prey to that temptation often miss out on some great returns from underappreciated funds. If a fund is hot enough to catch investors' attention, many of its holdings may sport tremendously high price multiples. Investors chasing such hot funds can wind up losing money when the companies they hold fail to live up to the lofty expectations embedded in their prices.

Take T. Rowe Price Media & Telecom, a top-notch sector fund. The offering boasted fantastic returns when the communications frenzy took hold in the late 1990s, posting a 93% gain in 1999. Investors loved the sector and they hopped on board just in time to spend the next three years in the red. It's worth pointing out, of course, that the fund continues to impress—at least on a relative basis. It may lose a lot of money from time to time, but it generally outpaces its industry rivals nicely.

Sector funds can often come with hefty price tags, even if the fund's sponsoring family isn't known for high fees. Be sure to examine the fund's fee structure, and don't pay too much.	**A warning**

If you can't resist the temptation to bet on a sector, though, do one of two things: Either play long-term trends (the aging of the baby boomers and increased demand for healthcare is one such trend) and dollar-cost average (invest a set dollar amount each month) into your sector fund, or make a bet on an out-of-favor sector, particularly one that most other fund investors are avoiding. Because the average investor doesn't have such good timing, you can often outperform by buying what most investors are selling. We'll explore this strategy in a later lesson.

A Few More Questions

In addition to the questions you would ask about performance, risk, portfolio holdings, management, and costs before buying any fund, ask two more questions that apply specifically to sector funds:

How diversified is it? As we explored earlier, some sector funds are quite concentrated. It's therefore important to know if the fund favors certain subsectors and totally disregards others.

To get some idea of a fund's diversification, you can use the Data Interpreter that's available on each fund's Fund Report on Morningstar.com. The Data Interpreter will give subsector breakdowns and note other risks of the fund. (Premium members can check out the in-depth Fund Analyses as well.) In addition, examine the portfolio holdings and a shareholder report. Finally, read the fund's prospectus.

Does it charge a redemption fee? Sector funds very often charge redemption fees if you sell the fund within a certain period of time from purchase. Redemption-fee information appears in the Fees and Expenses section of our Fund Reports.

As a long-term investor, you shouldn't get hung up on redemption fees, though. In fact, think of them as your friends. The fees penalize people who invest for less than a set period of time (often three months, but sometimes a year or more). Basically, they are penalties for early withdrawal that are paid back into the fund rather than to the fund company. Funds use these fees to deter investors who rush into hot funds, then flee when they turn cold. These shareholders can undermine a fund's performance with untimely buying and selling.

Fearless Facts

▶ Know what you own: Examine your portfolio using a diagnostic tool such as Morningstar's Instant X-Ray. This tool will demonstrate for you just how your portfolio shakes out in terms of sector exposure.

▶ Ready for the next step? Say you're low on computer software stocks and you like the looks of that industry. You might want to consider some specialty-technology funds. On the other hand, if your fund is full of growth companies specializing in all that's new, go for a modest natural-resources or utilities offering.

▶ Be realistic. Very few investors actually need sector funds. After all, your core portfolio should do a good job of diversifying your assets across industries and investing styles.

▶ Limit your exposure to sector funds. No investor needs to devote more than 5% of his or her portfolio to speculative sector investing.

▶ Don't go with the flow. The sector funds that usually catch our eye are the ones that are already on their way up. Try not to be a performance-chaser. Instead, focus on an industry that's underrepresented in your portfolio or that you know a lot about.

▶ Beware of expenses. Sector funds can be some of the most expensive offerings around. That's because fund shops don't want performance to be hurt by fickle investors, so they sometimes tack on very high redemption fees.

Quiz

1   Which statement is false?

Answers to this quiz can be found on page 273

   a   All investors need sector funds.

   b   You can use sector funds to diversify a portfolio.

   c   You can use sector funds to speculate on a particular industry.

2   Which sector-fund strategy should you avoid?

   a   Buying sector funds representing areas of the market in which you are currently underweighted.

   b   Buying sector funds that are performing exceptionally well.

   c   Buying sector funds that are unpopular with mutual fund investors.

3   What costs are actually good for long-term sector-fund investors?

   a   Annual expenses.

   b   Sales charges or loads.

   c   Redemption fees.

4   Which type of fund is bound to be most volatile?

   a   A fund investing only in Internet stocks.

   b   A fund investing in technology stocks, including Internet stocks.

   c   A fund investing in technology and nontechnology stocks.

5   If you're investing in a long-term trend, such as buying a health-care fund to play the Aging of America theme, which should you not do?

   a   Sell the fund if it loses money in a calendar year.

   b   Dollar-cost average into the fund.

   c   Buy when the sector is out of favor.

Worksheet

Why might an investor want to buy a sector fund?

What sectors might you consider investing in? What are your reasons for choosing that sector?

Now look at some of the funds that focus only on that sector. What are the key differences among them? Compare their expenses, concentration levels, and management tenures.

What is the maximum percentage of your portfolio that you would consider devoting to a sector fund?

Sector funds are often associated with market-timing because investors typically invest when they think a sector is hot and try to get out before it cools off. Do you agree with this investment strategy? Do you think sector funds make good long-term investments? Why or why not?

Lesson 306: Using Quirky Bond Funds

We've just talked about using various types of funds that can add value to a portfolio. We covered growth funds and value funds, focused and flexible funds, even sector funds. But let's not forget about bond funds.

We'll talk about more than your grandmother's T-bills here; we'll explore high-yield bond funds, bank-loan funds, and inflation-indexed bond funds. These funds are designed to stamp out some of the interest-rate or inflation risk that may lurk elsewhere in your portfolio. You can also buy them to pick up some extra return.

High-Yield, or Junk, Bond Funds

If you are looking to expand your bond-fund horizons, high yield may be the first area you've considered. High-yield bonds are often called lower-quality bonds, or junk bonds. No matter the name, these bonds offer much more income than Treasuries or other high-quality corporate bonds. That's because they have more credit risk—the risk that their issuers may not be able to make regular income payments or pony up the principal they originally promised to return. In other words, if the economy slows down, or if the companies fall into trouble, they may not be able to pay back the IOU.

Because credit risk, not interest-rate risk, is their Achilles' heel, junk bonds help diversify the interest-rate risk inherent with most high-quality bonds. Remember, funds favoring high-grade bonds with far-off maturities can be pretty volatile, depending on what interest rates do. But because junk bonds pay higher yields and are often denominated in shorter maturities, they aren't as sensitive to interest-rate shifts as higher-quality, longer-duration bonds are. For example, 2004 has been a year of rising rates and the promise of more rate hikes. But the average junk-bond fund, which is far less vulnerable to interest-rate movements, has gained 3.06% through August, affected more by declining defaults and improving corporate profits.

When shopping for a junk-bond fund, examine a fund's credit quality, which appears on our Fund Reports. Is the fund investing in the upper tiers of junk (say, bonds with credit qualities of BB and B), or is it dipping lower for added yield? Check, too, to see if the fund owns any stock, convertible bonds (bonds that convert to stocks), or bonds from emerging markets. These elements would likely make the fund more volatile. Finally, examine how the fund performed during tough markets for junk-bond funds. That will give you a sense of how risky the fund could be in the future. Those tough markets will be periods when the economy faltered. Junk-bond investors experienced trying periods in 1990 and during the summer of 2002 (when Worldcom's bankruptcy roiled the high-yield market).

Keep in mind that high-yield bond funds can be a good supplement to a portfolio already well rounded with Treasuries, corporate bonds, and mortgages, all of which offer high credit quality. But you'll generally want to keep junk to less than one-fourth of your bond assets.

Bank-Loan Funds

There's almost no better place to pick up a lot of income with low volatility than with bank-loan funds (also known as prime-rate funds). As their name makes clear, these funds invest in bank loans. Banks typically make such loans to companies (most of which have poor credit profiles) as part of a leveraged buyout deal, and then they sell these loans to institutional investors and mutual funds. The yields on the loans rise and fall along with interest rates, which helps cushion the effect of interest-rate changes on the funds' NAVs.

We often think of bond funds as a place of refuge when equity markets turn south. This isn't necessarily the case with the junk-bond market. Higher-yielding debt sometimes behaves more like stocks than other bonds; in the past several years, funds buying low credit quality bonds have done well in go-growth markets and have struggled during economic slowdowns. Thus, junk shouldn't be used as a diversification tool for an equity-heavy portfolio.

Not your typical bonds

Sound too good to be true? In some ways, it is. In fact, bank-loan funds come with plenty of caveats. First, most charge relatively high fees when compared with the average bond fund. Further, some use investment leverage, which boosts gains but also magnifies losses. Leverage is essentially borrowing to invest. Say a fund with $100 million in assets invests those assets in a security returning 10% over a given period. In addition, it borrows another $25 million, which it invests in the same security with the same 10% return. At the end of the period, the fund will have increased in value by $12.5 million

(10% of $125 million), representing a 12.5% return on the $100 million of its own assets invested by the fund, greater than the 10% the fund would have earned had it not borrowed the $25 million. However, if the securities the fund holds were to fall by 10% instead of rising by 10%, it would be left with a loss of 12.5% rather than the loss of 10% that an unleveraged fund would have endured.

The biggest drawback to bank-loan funds, however, are the restrictive redemption policies most have. Because the market for corporate loans is so tiny, it's tough for bank-loan funds to sell these loans to meet shareholder redemptions. Therefore, most bank-loan funds will allow investors to sell their shares only on a quarterly basis. (You can, however, buy at any time.) And if too many people want to cash out when you do, you may not be able to sell as many shares as you would like.

Though bank-loan funds display less sensitivity to interest-rate shifts than many bond funds, that doesn't mean they can't lose money. In fact, most bank-loan funds were nicked by slight principal losses in 1999, thanks to some shaky loans. But these funds can nonetheless provide ballast to your portfolio.

When examining bank-loan funds, be sure you understand the funds' redemption policies, and know whether you can tie up your money for as long as is required by the fund. Watch costs. And be sure you know whether or not the fund uses leverage.

Inflation-Indexed Bond Funds

Inflation-indexed bonds are the holy grail of income investing: limited volatility and a guarantee that your fund won't get ravaged by high inflation.

The value of an inflation-indexed bond rises with inflation, and inflation's something that's almost as certain as death and taxes. Conversely, an inflation-indexed bond's value can fall in a deflationary climate, but not usually below the bond's face or par value. Inflation-indexed bonds won't perform very well when inflation looks tame and conventional bonds are zooming up in price, but that diversification effect is part of the appeal.

Most funds focusing on inflation-indexed bonds stick with the highest quality, or those issued by the U.S. Treasury, which are commonly referred to as TIPS. There are also a small number of other bonds issued by government agencies and corporations that try to keep pace with inflation.

At the end of 1999, there were only a handful of dedicated inflation-indexed bond funds out there, including PIMCO Real Return and American Century Inflation-Adjusted Treasury. But in recent years investors have clamored for these types of securities, spawning a host of other offerings which hope to ride the TIPS wave.

Pulling It All Together

Ultimately, the key to bond-fund investing is understanding what your funds can and can't do. A basic high-quality fund can act as a good balance to a stock portfolio, but by its very nature it shouldn't be expected to outperform stocks over a long period of time. (High-quality bonds offer much more certain returns than stocks, so they don't have to proffer such high returns to attract investors.) And because interest rates almost never stand still, a bond fund shouldn't be expected to turn in positive returns every single year, either. That's where bonds with different structures, such as TIPS, or those with some credit sensitivity, such as junk bonds, can prove to be a welcome elixir.

Buy for the Right Reason

Your Worry	Bond Rx
Declining buying power of the dollar—inflation!	Inflation-protected bonds (such as TIPS)
Rising interest rates	Shorter-term bonds
Interest-rate volatility	Junk bonds; bank loans
Default	Higher-quality bonds
I don't care about interest rate-risk; I just want some income!	Mortgage-backed bonds

Bonds are great protection from whatever's bothering you. But if you get into the fixed-income world for heady returns, you're likely to be disappointed. Above, a quick rundown of your possible worries and the bond prescription that can cure your cares.

Fearless Facts

▶ If you're worried about interest-rate risk in your existing bond fund, you might want to try your hand in the junk-bond market.

▶ Just as concerned about credit risk? Look for higher-quality shorter-term bond funds and steer clear of junk-bond offerings.

▶ Are you panicked about the declining power of the U.S. dollar? If inflation has you running scared, you'll want to look at inflation-indexed bonds. Government bonds that are inflation-indexed are called TIPS (Treasury Inflation Protected Securities).

▶ Emerging-markets bond funds should not be considered part of the fixed-income portion of your portfolio. That's because these offerings don't usually respond to changes in the U.S. interest-rate environment the way domestic bond offerings do. Sure, emerging-markets bonds share traits with certain junk offerings (including very low credit ratings). But these funds are dependent on the macro-economic and political developments in their home countries. Thus, they should be treated as part of the international portion of your portfolio.

Quiz

1   Which type of fund would not likely offset interest-rate risk elsewhere in your portfolio?

a	High-quality bond fund.
b	High-yield fund.
c	Prime-rate fund.

Answers to this quiz can be found on page 273

2   Which type of fund should fare best if inflation rises?

a	High-yield bond fund.
b	High-quality bond fund.
c	Inflation-indexed bond fund.

3   Which type of fund does *not* have much credit risk?

a	High-yield bond fund.
b	Prime-rate fund.
c	Inflation-indexed bond fund.

4   Which type of fund owns senior bank loans, or loans from low-quality companies?

a	High-yield bond fund.
b	Prime-rate fund.
c	Inflation-indexed bond fund.

5   Which type of fund will probably suffer most in an economic slowdown?

a	Prime-rate fund.
b	Inflation-indexed bond fund.
c	High-yield bond fund.

Worksheet

Have you ever invested in junk-bond funds, bank-loan funds, or inflation-indexed funds? If so, what were your reasons for doing so?

What are some disadvantages of bank loan-funds? What characteristics of these funds do you think are appealing?

Why do some market watchers consider inflation-indexed funds to be almost risk-free? Do you agree with that assessment? How might a TIPS fund help diversify your bond portfolio's risk?

Some investment pros say that junk-bond funds might not be an effective way to diversify a stock-fund-heavy portfolio. Why do you think this might be the case?

Troubleshoot Portfolio Problem Areas

Lesson 307: Bear-Proofing Your Portfolio

The investing world's jargon is sometimes too colorful. For example, there are "bull markets," or periods in which a particular type of investment does exceptionally well. Less pleasantly, there are "bear markets," or times when a particular type of investment performs poorly.

Now if only we knew when those bears would roar, or what investments would survive the mauling. But because each slump brings its own new twists, yesterday's bear-market hero may not survive the next downturn nearly as well. Besides, even if bear-proofing a portfolio were simple, it may not be smart.

A Bear Is Not a Bear Is Not a Bear

Over the past 20 years, the Dow Jones Industrial Average has slid by 20% a handful of times. That means if you had $100 invested before the slide, it was worth $80 at the end. Each bear attacked in different ways, but there have been some common themes. Technology funds and natural-resources funds, for example, have been struck repeatedly. On the other hand, income-oriented utilities and investment-grade bond funds typically escape major trauma.

Everything else has been less predictable. Small-company funds held up well during one bear market, then suffered during the next one. Junk-bond funds have wandered all over the map, posting gains in the early bear markets but collapsing in 1990 as the economy weakened and stumbling again from 2000 to 2002 amid a spate of downgrades and defaults in the energy, cable and telecom areas. Gold has also been mixed: Anyone who came out of the late-1970s bear market believing gold was the place to be on a long-term basis got burned in the early 1980s, when the bear knocked precious-metals funds for a 30% loss. In recent years, however, gold has provided a haven for investors fearing inflation and geopolitical instability. In the new century, cautious investors have flooded the precious-metals category.

Funds That Produced the Best Dollar-Weighted Returns

Fund Name	Bull Market Cumulative* Return %	Bear Market Dollar Weighted Annlzd Return %	Total Annlzd Return %
Wasatch Core Growth WGROX	21.21	30.01	15.11
Wasatch Micro Cap WMICX	58.08	24.34	26.32
Bjurman, Barry Micro Cap Growth BMCFX	71.45	21.12	24.01
Calamos Growth ACVGRX	126.23	17.88	21.39
Sentinel Small Company A SAGWX	23.36	15.33	14.03
Columbia Acorn ZACRNX	41.41	13.74	13.65
Wasatch ULTRA Growth WAMCX	46.60	12.08	15.64
Wasatch Small Cap Growth WAAEX	56.61	11.12	15.21
Columbia Acorn USA Z AUSAX	30.14	10.17	10.17
T. Rowe Price Mid Cap Growth RPMGX	51.01	9.73	10.37

Data through August 31, 2004. *Cumulative Returns from 1988 and 1989

Funds with more modest published returns during the latter stages of the bull market often delivered the best actual showings for investors. (Dollar-weighted returns measure the returns that investors actually experienced, based on the timing of their purchase and sales.)

Three Varieties of Bear

Many different causes can trigger a bear market, but usually the cause has something to do with the economy. Here are three common causes of bear markets, as well as what types of investments tend to do best in each type of bear market.

Recession. A recession hit the U.S. in early 2000. That's when the air began to seep out of the tech bubble. The collapse of stock prices crimped the ability of speculative tech and Internet enterprises to use their pricey stock as the currency for acquisitions. What's more, business spending—the lifeblood of growth for many new economy names—slowed to a halt as companies pared back their budgets following the sizable outlays required to fix the Y2K problem and upgrade infrastructure to keep pace with more nimble upstarts.

While inflation remained in check and consumers continued to spend (thanks to near-record low interest rates, which spurred a wave of refinancings), the economy shrunk all the same.

Firms that deliver inexpensive or staple products, such as food, beverages, cigarettes, and health-care items, do well in a recessionary environment. Other stocks, such as automakers, steel producers, and paper manufacturers, are highly sensitive to economic cycles—hence they are termed cyclicals. Such stocks pop up most often in value funds. High-yield (or junk) bond funds can also be risky when the economy sours.

Rapid inflation. From the 1960s through the 1980s, many investors viewed inflation as a given. Not even common stocks could protect investors from the price increases of the late 1970s. During normal circumstances, large-company stocks will provide an annual return that outpaces inflation over the long term, but during the inflationary 1970s, even those stocks couldn't keep up with Treasury bills.

Frankly...	When it comes right down to it, we're not a fan of bear-market funds. Some attempt to time the market, and history suggests that very few managers can time the market correctly and consistently over a long period. Others are bearish all the time, which is a recipe for poor performance given that the long-term trend in equity prices is up. Finally, many of these offerings are expensive.

As a result, investors in the 1970s flocked to tangible assets such as real estate, art, and gold. Precious-metals funds posted four years of positive returns from 1977 to 1980, a feat they haven't repeated since. Today, real estate funds are the most popular inflation hedge, but other options exist. For example, inflation-indexed Treasury bonds offer income as well as inflation protection.

Everything else, including regular bonds and stocks not tied to some hard asset such as real estate, tends to lag during periods of rapid inflation.

Deflation. After the late-1997 troubles in Southeast Asian economies, deflation became the economic worry du jour in the United States. Pundits speculated that a flood of cheap Asian imports would force

U.S. companies to lower their own prices, sparking a general fall in the U.S. Consumer Price Index—or in other words, deflation. That situation hadn't occurred since the Great Depression in the 1930s, when overall prices declined by as much as 10% in a single year. For a variety of reasons, deflation makes it more difficult for businesses to grow their profits, thus weakening stock prices.

Long- and intermediate-term bond funds tend to hold up relatively well in this environment because their dividends are effectively worth more in this type of economy. A 6% dividend delivers more purchasing power each year if prices are falling by 2% annually. Among equities, look for dividend-rich stocks and the funds that own them.

What suffers? Inflation-indexed bonds, non–dividend-paying stocks, and anything tied to a real asset such as gold or real estate do poorly in a deflationary environment. Remember, deflation means a decline in the prices of tangible assets.

What to Do?

Preparing for a bear market is clearly a vexing problem, given the variety of bears. Here is what we think:

Don't try to time the market by switching to cash. Anyone who tries to trick the bear by selling investments and piling up cash will likely suffer less-than-perfect timing and miss out on big stock-market gains.

Unless you know something we don't or are extremely lucky, you won't get rich playing the timing game.

Recognize the limitations of bonds and gold. Given that utilities and bond funds have evaded the bear in a number of situations, they might be decent shelters. There are some caveats, though. For one, tucking too much money in these bear-market champs is a good way to avoid bull markets, too. During the bull market of the 1990s, bonds and utilities didn't return nearly as much as diversified domestic-equity funds did.

Moreover, these funds aren't completely bulletproof. For starters, being better than everyone else isn't the same as being good. Bonds may have been the best thing going in 1990, but they still lost money as the Persian Gulf crisis unfolded and interest rates spiked. Also, keep in mind that these funds do endure their own separate bear markets from time to time; investors learned that the hard way in 1994, when utilities funds plunged 9% in an otherwise flat market.

Be wary of committing to bear-market funds. An alternative to bond and utilities funds are funds designed specifically to battle the bear, called bear-market funds. These funds—which typically bet against stocks by shorting stock indexes or individual stocks—galloped to robust gains in the recent bear market. However, remember that bull markets won't likely be kind to these funds. It's also worth noting that stocks have increased in value over long periods of time, and bear markets tend to be relatively brief in historical terms. Using a bear-market fund effectively requires that you be able to predict when the market is going to head south, and few, if any investors, have shown any ability to do this consistently.

Grin and bear it. Let's face it: Investing has its risks, one of which is losing money. It's going to happen from time to time. Diversifying across a variety of fund types and asset classes won't prevent the blow, but it will soften it. Every bear leaves at least a few fund categories with relatively minor injuries.

After setting up a diversified portfolio that meshes with your long-term goals, the best plan is the most obvious one. Stay the course, invest regularly, and promise yourself not to panic when (not if) the market stumbles. The prospect may seem unappealing, but the alternatives can be worse.

Fearless Facts

▶ Recession is a downturn in economic activity. It's defined by economists as at least two consecutive quarters of declining GDP.

▶ A bear market is typically defined as a 20% drop in the value of a given asset class.

▶ Inflation is an increase in the general price level of services and goods or a decline in the purchasing power of the dollar.

▶ Deflation is a decline in the general price level of services and goods or an increase in the purchasing power of the dollar. It may be good for you, the consumer, at least for a little while. However, deflation robs companies of their pricing power, so there's a good chance that your stock portfolio will suffer.

Quiz

1 During a bear market:

a	A particular type of investment performs poorly.
b	Inflation rises.
c	There is a recession.

Answers to this quiz can be found on page 274

2 During a recessionary period, what usually holds up well?

a	Junk bonds.
b	Cyclical stocks.
c	Health-care stocks.

3 During a period of rapid inflation, what usually holds up well?

a	Gold.
b	Large-company stocks.
c	Regular bonds.

4 During a period of deflation, what usually holds up well?

a	Gold.
b	Bonds.
c	Stocks without dividends.

5 What's the best way to bear-proof a portfolio?

a	Move into cash when you think a bear is coming.
b	Buy only bear-market funds.
c	Build a diverse portfolio that owns a little bit of everything.

Worksheet

If you were investing during the bear market from 2000 through 2002, did you learn any lessons from that experience? Have you taken any steps to adjust your portfolio in the wake of the bear market?

In a recession, why are cyclical companies often hit the hardest? What types of companies might best help you avoid losses during a recession?

What are bear-market funds and what do they have to offer investors? Does such a fund appeal to you? Why or why not?

Do you think that diversifying your portfolio and staying the course is the best option? Why or why not? If not, what would you do instead?

Lesson 308: The Plight of the Fickle Investor

In investing, three truths are held to be self-evident:

1 Investors should buy low and sell high.
2 Investors should not be propelled by panic.
3 Investors should not assume past performance guarantees future results.

Or at least that's what everybody says. What fund investors actually do is another matter entirely. They are often fickle, buying funds that have done well (or buying high) and selling in a panic when they stall (that is, selling low). In doing so, investors sabotage their own results. Here's what not to do.

The Tale of PBHG Growth

The classic case of buy high and sell low has to be PBHG Growth. From 1992 through 1995, the fund quietly built a superb record, though it wasn't attracting a lot of attention (or cash inflows) from new investors. In early 1996, when the fund's average three-year gain of more than 30% placed it on many a leader's list, the money started rolling in. Nearly $2.5 billion poured in during the first six months of 1996, just in time for the fund's 10% slide in July. New money slowed. Then, in early 1997, after the fund had suffered several months of losses, shareholders started bailing out, missing a strong second-quarter rebound.

History Repeats Itself

Although few funds have cash-flow stories as dramatic as PBHG Growth's, Morningstar studies have found that investors across all fund types—both stocks and bonds—have paid a price for being fickle.

The damage is greater on the stock-fund side, especially with aggressive funds, in which volatility and temptation are highest. In the small-growth category, for example, one Morningstar study found that investors had surrendered 1.8 percentage points annually by chasing performance rather than by simply investing a little each month, or dollar-cost averaging. It's not surprising that the small- and mid-cap growth categories have been land mines for investors. It's easy to get caught up in the excitement of a go-go fund's performance. Don't-don't.

Control yourself

One of the surest ways to get into trouble is by chasing returns. A little pre-planning can make a big difference when it comes to investing temptations.

1. Plan ahead. At the beginning of the year (or at tax time), decide how much cash you're willing to devote to investing over the course of the next 12 months.

2. Design a long-term investment program to meet your investment goals with an acceptable level of risk, and stick to it.

3. If you really want to, set aside a small portion of your portfolio for short-term moves. This should be no more than 5% of your overall portfolio, and it should be a sum you can afford to lose.

Clearly, emotion has a way of interfering with reason. That's why dollar-cost averaging can be such a good idea. Sure, it's possible to make more money with a lump-sum investment. But it's also possible to make less.

The Lessons

What can fickle mutual fund investors teach you?

Discipline generally pays. Because emotions and hype can get in the way of smart investing, systematic dollar-cost averaging is a sound strategy. Granted, investing a lump sum in the market as soon as you have the cash can be a good approach when the markets just keep going up, or when you are certain you won't give in to the temptation to buy or sell at the wrong time. But in many cases, the dollar-cost averager is going to beat the willy-nilly investor.

Don't try to navigate a minefield. Discipline is particularly important in riskier areas, in which the hope for big gains and the reality of big losses can tempt even well-meaning investors into making trading blunders. If you invest in aggressive funds, promise yourself you won't back out when returns head south. If the manager and strategy that you originally bought are still there, you should be, too.

Don't chase funds. Of course, even levelheaded, systematic investors need to alter their portfolios from time to time. When moving money or picking new funds, resist the temptation to chase performance. If anything, invest in areas everyone else is ignoring.

Fearless Facts

 First, a review of the Morningstar mantra:
- ▶ Buy low, sell high.
- ▶ No panic.
- ▶ Don't expect the future to repeat the past.

Morningstar has found that dollar-cost averaging is one of the best—and most successful—ways to invest money over a longer time period.

If you're determined to be aggressive, commit ahead of time. In other words, before jumping into that hot fund with sky-high returns, choose a time frame that you're comfortable with (always more than a year) and stick it out over that period, even if performance heads south.

Quiz

1   Fickle investors sabotage their investment returns by:

Answers to this quiz can be found on page 274

a	Buying funds when they are hot and selling them when they turn cold.
b	Buying funds when they are cold and selling them when they are hot.
c	Investing a little bit at a time.

2   Which fund types treat fickle investors the worst?

a	Bond funds.
b	Large-company funds.
c	Small- and mid-cap growth funds.

3   If you are afraid of becoming a fickle investor, you should:

a	Dollar-cost average into funds.
b	Make lump-sum investments.
c	Try to time the market.

4   If you have new money to invest and you want to invest in an aggressive fund, Morningstar would most likely say:

a	Invest it all at once.
b	Invest a little at a time.
c	Wait for the fund to cool, then buy.

5   Which is not one of the three truths of investing?

a	Investors should buy low and sell high.
b	Investors should not be propelled by panic.
c	Investors should assume past performance guarantees future results.

Worksheet

Why do you think investors chase performance? Have you done that in the past? Did you end up making money, or would you have been better off staying put in the investments you started out with?

Why should you be particularly wary of investing in the next hot thing?

Why do you think so many investors have trouble sticking to a long-term investing plan?

Lesson 309: Chasing Closed Funds

We've all done it. There's a bank of six elevators, yet we'll risk life, limb, and cups of coffee to board the one whose doors are closing. Heaven forbid we wait a whole 10 seconds for the next one to arrive. Fund investors do the same thing. They hear that a fund is going to stop accepting money from new investors in a few days, weeks, or months, and they immediately write a check, as if there's no other fund that could possibly meet their needs.

Of course, fund closings have their merits. Funds close so their managers can continue to invest in their given styles; too many assets can force managers to compromise their strategies. However, there's no evidence that rushing the doors of a soon-to-close fund is a good idea. Here's what Morningstar has found, and why fund closings aren't always the magic elixirs they are cracked up to be.

Performance Takes a Hit

In a recent study, Morningstar examined the performance of 38 funds that closed during a 15-year period. Specifically, we measured performance in the three-year periods before and after the fund's closing. We define closed as barring new investors. Most closed funds allow existing shareholders to send more money, however, so closed funds often continue to get big inflows after closing.

For every fund that saw its relative performance improve, three more suffered a decline in the three years after they closed. On average, closed funds' returns relative to their peer groups fell from top quintile in the three years before their closings to slightly below average in the three years after.

Does that mean closing a fund actually does damage? No. In fact, the performance slump probably has little to do with closing. The explanation is simply that hot funds usually cool off. While a fund may get steady inflows over most of its life, the point at which it closes is usually when inflows become a torrent. And that almost always happens when a fund's strategy or asset class is generating abnormally high returns. Pick any strategy that's producing big returns for a stretch, and it's a good bet performance will slide back to average or worse over the following period.

Take Janus Olympus. It produced a staggering 57.5% annualized return over the three years prior to its May 2000 closing. However, it closed just as large-growth stocks were peaking and subsequently spun to a 32.7% annualized loss from its closing until it eventually reopened in August 2002. The general performance drop-off for closed funds stands more as further evidence against chasing short-term performance than as an argument against closing. Still, it's sobering to know that a fund's best days are often behind it by the time it closes.

Another reason why closed funds produce sluggish performance is that fund companies fail to close funds until performance hits the skids or assets are gargantuan. By then, it's too late. If performance is already slumping, then it may be a sign it should have closed billions of dollars ago. Closing off new investment won't slim a fund down to its playing weight from its glory days.

It's reasonable to want to chase closed funds: After all, a fund that shuts its doors indicates that it has the best interests of its current shareholders at heart. But keep in mind that there's often another way to play. Many closed funds are run by managers who have a stable of other solid offerings.

Second best is sometimes good enough

... and Taxes Make It Worse

Performance isn't the only factor eroding returns of closed funds. Their tax efficiency often slumps, too. Unlike the drop in performance, however, declining tax efficiency is attributable to the closing itself. While inflows can make trading more difficult, they have a positive effect on tax efficiency. They reduce the tax burden on all shareholders because there are more shareholders to distribute capital gains across. Morningstar found that the average closed fund's tax efficiency fell five percentage points after its closing date.

It's worth noting, though, that tax considerations have played a part in at least one fund company's decision-making process on closing funds. Vanguard has closed a few funds from time to time, including

Primecap, but it has left a number of big funds open. Vanguard officials say that the negative tax consequences of closing outweigh the pluses. Rather than close funds such as Explorer, Vanguard has added more managers.

Is Closing Bad, Then?

Closing a fund can enable a manager to stick with the investment strategy that has brought him or her success in the past: Excessive assets typically force a change in strategy, a problem we'll explore in greater detail later. Closing is still probably worthwhile for funds with a small number of managers and analysts, a strategy sensitive to asset size, such as high-turnover momentum investing, or a fund that focuses on a less liquid asset class, such as small caps or real estate investment trusts (REITs).

Moreover, a number of fund companies have developed what appear to be effective game plans for closing new funds even before they are rolled out. They make their own estimate of what asset size would be appropriate for the fund and sometimes even make a public pledge to close when assets hit a certain level. (Most of these funds closed before they built a three-year record and were thus excluded from our study of closed funds' performance.) The initial signs from this group of early closers are positive.

Wasatch serves as a good example of this. Through the years, this small-cap boutique has paid strict attention to fund size to ward against asset bloat. For instance, in January 2002, Wasatch shuttered its Small-Cap Value offering to new investors only to reopen its doors nine months later. However, when assets poured in, the firm didn't dawdle, closing the fund to new investors again at the end of 2002. In mid-2004, it's still closed. That vigilance appears to have paid off as Wasatch funds' stellar performance through the years owes at least partly to their manageable size.

Wait. And Other Helpful Hints

Many of the funds that have closed at some point in the past 20 years have later reopened. Fidelity Magellan and Fidelity Low-Priced Stock have each closed a few times. The same hot money that forces sizzling funds to shut sometimes flees the fund when performance cools, leading funds to reopen their doors. In fact, reopening might be a sign that an asset class is being overlooked and is worth a second look.

Besides watching for reopened funds, keep an eye out for new funds that promise to close at a point when they still have reasonably sized asset bases. But you still need to make sure that it has all the basics of a good fund: strong management, a good strategy, and low costs. If it doesn't, take a pass. There are thousands of open funds, and at least a few ought to meet your needs.

Fearless Facts

▶ We all want to join the clubs that won't have us, but keep in mind that a closing fund isn't necessarily a great fund.

▶ Remember, Morningstar's research suggests that funds often close late in the game, after assets are already large. Thus, closings are often followed by a dip in performance.

▶ Look before you leap: Be aware that a closing fund means fewer shareholders. Fewer shareholders mean more capital gains per investor. More capital gains for investors means more taxes for you. If you're just jumping into a fund, you may not have received all the benefits of great performance—but you'll still foot some of that tax bill!

▶ It isn't such a bad thing to take a pass on a closing fund. After all, there's a good chance the offering will reopen; furthermore, you're likely to find a comparable fund out there.

Quiz

1   Which is not true about many funds after they close?

Answers to this quiz can be found on page 275

> **a**   Their returns often slow down.
>
> **b**   Their tax efficiency improves.
>
> **c**   Their tax efficiency worsens.

2   Why do a closed fund's returns often slow down after the closing?

> **a**   Because closings are bad.
>
> **b**   Because funds that closed are usually experiencing abnormally high returns that must eventually come back down to earth.
>
> **c**   Because there's no new money coming in.

3   Closings work best for which types of funds?

> **a**   High-turnover funds.
>
> **b**   Large-company funds.
>
> **c**   Foreign funds.

4   If a fund is going to close, what's the best way to do it?

> **a**   Announce a target asset size and close when it reaches that target.
>
> **b**   Close once assets top $10 billion.
>
> **c**   Close once inflows become unmanageable.

5   It's best to:

> **a**   Buy a fund before it closes.
>
> **b**   Buy a fund after it reopens.
>
> **c**   Sell a fund after it reopens.

Worksheet

Have you ever bought a fund right before it closed? Did the fund fit your investment profile?

Why do you think funds that close often post disappointing performance in the years after they close?

Have you ever owned a fund that closed? In your experience, has performance or tax efficiency dropped dramatically after your fund closed?

Why do you think it might be a good idea to invest in funds and fund families that have announced a preset asset level at which they'll close?

Lesson 310: Buying the Unloved

It can be hard to turn your back on a winner. Investors usually flock to those parts of the market with great returns. But chances are, those stellar returns won't last forever. Sears is no longer the nation's preeminent retailer, *I Love Lucy* is no longer a top prime-time sitcom, and few of us are still walking around in poodle skirts.

Play against the crowd, though, and you just may catch a future trend today. Fund investors, as a group, have lousy timing. Most investors buy high and sell low, instead of the other way around. Opportunists can therefore make a bundle by buying what everyone else is selling.

So here's how to be an opportunist, the Morningstar way.

Morningstar's Unpopularity Contest

At the end of every year, we find the three most unpopular fund categories of the year based on percentage change in cash flows, or how much money is going into and out of mutual funds. We then recommend that you buy one fund from each unpopular category and stick with them for three years.

Morningstar back-tested this strategy to 1987 and found winning results. Unpopular categories beat the average equity fund more than three-fourths of the time. The results versus popular categories have been even better. Unpopular categories topped the popular ones over the next three years more than 80% of the time. Investing doesn't get much closer to a sure thing than that.

Unpopular Categories Tend to Beat Popular Categories and the Average Fund

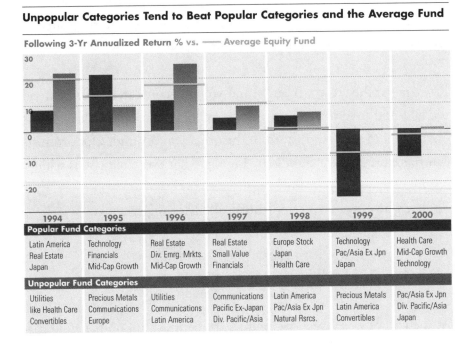

Following 3-Yr Annualized Return % vs. —— Average Equity Fund

	1994	1995	1996	1997	1998	1999	2000
Popular Fund Categories							
	Latin America Real Estate Japan	Technology Financials Mid-Cap Growth	Real Estate Div. Emrg. Mrkts. Mid-Cap Growth	Real Estate Small Value Financials	Europe Stock Japan Health Care	Technology Pac/Asia Ex Jpn Japan	Health Care Mid-Cap Growth Technology
Unpopular Fund Categories							
	Utilities like Health Care Convertibles	Precious Metals Communications Europe	Utilities Communications Latin America	Communications Pacific Ex-Japan Div. Pacific/Asia	Latin America Pac/Asia Ex Jpn Natural Rsrcs.	Precious Metals Latin America Convertibles	Pac/Asia Ex Jpn Div. Pacific/Asia Japan

The Rules

Putting our unpopular-categories strategy into action is simple. In fact, there are just three rules to follow:

Buy one fund from each category. Staking everything on just one unpopular category can be risky. Not every unloved category will catch fire, and one category can pull the weight for the entire group. The unpopular categories from 1996, for instance, averaged a roughly 25% annualized return for the three subsequent years, but the communications category's 46.6% annualized return was crucial to that performance.

Buy before summer vacation. After examining category returns for the three-year holding period minus one month, minus two months, and so on, we found that there's not much of a penalty for lateness. Most of the time, you could buy the unpopular categories as much as a year after reading our story and the strategy still worked. We would rather err on the side of caution, though. Buying the funds at the beginning of June worked as well as buying them in January, so just be sure to purchase by midyear. If you buy later, your odds of success will be lower.

Limit your bets. Resist the urge to put more than 5% of your portfolio into unpopular categories. That way you'll minimize the disappointment in one of those rare occasions when the strategy doesn't work. We advocated holding precious metals, Latin America, and convertibles funds from 2000 through 2002, for example. Though precious-metals funds galloped to an impressive 16.9% annualized return, the story wasn't as happy for investors in Latin America or convertibles offerings, which have tumbled 13.6% and 5% respectively during that time. You can minimize risk in such situations by investing only 5% of your portfolio into unpopular categories.

Three Ways to Use the Strategy

Invest new money. Maybe your company paid you a nice bonus this year, or maybe you have some cash you have been sitting on. Put that money to work by buying one fund from each of our unpopular categories for the year.

Are we changing our tune?	This isn't an approach that will appeal to most investors. It's for those people who like to take a chance now and again and who are vigilant about their portfolios. After all, this approach requires at least a three-year commitment—the buying phase (between January and June) and the selling phase (three years later). If you're not dying to trade, this isn't an approach we recommend.

Sell one, buy the other. If you are strapped for cash, try taking gains on popular fund categories and shifting the gains into out-of-favor categories.

Cut back on the favorites. You'll do yourself a favor by simply reducing your exposure to popular categories. Had you followed this advice in early 1998, you would have avoided real estate and small-value funds' losses of 16% and 7%, respectively, and financials' subpar 6% gain in 1998. None of those categories did better than mark time in 1999. However, don't automatically sell funds in popular categories. If you do, you might suffer ugly tax consequences, as well as mess up your asset allocation.

Look for Morningstar's list of popular and unpopular categories in *Morningstar FundInvestor* and *Morningstar Mutual Funds* (available in many libraries) in early February of each year.

Fearless Facts

▶ If you're going to follow Morningstar's (Un)Popularity Contest, you'll need to be vigilant.

▶ Check out *Morningstar FundInvestor* or *Morningstar Mutual Funds* (found in many libraries) in early February to find the results of Morningstar's research. We'll let you know what the three least popular asset classes were in the past year: Usually, these asset classes have experienced significant outflows (shareholder redemptions).

▶ Buy one fund from each category—but not just any fund. Look for those funds with good records within their categories and that sport reasonable expenses. Plus, be sure to look at the fund's sales charges, too. After all, this is a trading strategy, so you need to know what you'll pay to move into and out of the funds.

▶ Buy early. Of course we don't want you to buy before you've done your homework. However, we've back-tested this strategy assuming that investors picked up funds before the midyear point (June).

▶ Most importantly, limit your bets. We don't think any investors should devote more than 5% of their portfolios to this strategy.

Quiz

1   Morningstar's unpopular-funds strategy works because:

a	Most fund investors have lousy timing.
b	Most fund investors have good timing.
c	Unpopular funds stay unpopular.

Answers to this quiz can be found on page 275

2   Unpopular categories are categories:

a	That have poor returns.
b	That don't have much money going into them.
c	That have terrific returns.

3   To improve your odds:

a	Buy one fund from one of the unpopular categories.
b	Buy one fund from each of the three unpopular categories.
c	Buy after June.

4   You should put how much of your assets into unpopular categories?

a	No more than five percent.
b	Twenty-five percent.
c	As much as you want.

5   What should you do about popular categories?

a	Buy more of them.
b	Sell them, no matter what.
c	Consider cutting back on them.

Worksheet

Have you ever invested in an unpopular sector or fund category, hoping to catch the bottom and ride the wave to the top? If so, did your hunch play out as you thought it would?

How much of your portfolio would you be willing to invest in this strategy? How can you work this strategy into your portfolio?

How similar is this strategy to the contrarian investing style of investors such as Warren Buffett?

Lesson 311: Buying Rookie Funds

Colonel Tom Parker had to be one of the smartest people in music history. He knew potential when he saw it. In 1954, Colonel Tom heard a young Elvis Presley singing on Louisiana Hayride, a live Saturday night country music show. He struck up a business relationship with Elvis, snagging some tour dates. Less than a year later, the Colonel took exclusive control of the King's career. The rest is history.

Every mutual fund investor hopes to spot up-and-coming mutual funds and get in on the ground floor of a great new investment. Granted, investing in a new fund is a gamble. Without Morningstar ratings and a few years of return and risk information as guides, how can you be sure you are getting the Next Big Thing? Nothing's certain, of course, so we suggest you ask the following questions before buying a new fund.

Has the Manager Run a Mutual Fund Before?

Favor new funds run by managers with some previous mutual fund experience, and be sure to scrutinize their records. Some prospectuses will include the manager's experience, while others won't. Check out the fund family's Web site for more information, or examine the fund's Fund Report, if available. (Morningstar doesn't always have Fund Reports for brand-new funds.) Be sure that the manager will be practicing a similar style at the new fund as he or she did with their previous fund.

What Kind of Record Does the Fund Family Have?

You might consider taking a chance on a fund run by a manager with no fund experience, but only if the fund family has a strong strategy or identity and a solid mutual fund history. A good fund family won't tolerate underperformance for long because it has a reputation to uphold. Also make sure that the new fund's manager has been with the family for a while and has internalized the family's investment approach.

You can check up on a family's entire roster of funds by typing the family's name in the Quotes & Reports box on Morningstar's home page.

What Is the Manager's Strategy?

You need to understand the manager's strategy to set realistic expectations for your investment. When the market does X, what can you expect from this fund? Also, when those inevitable dry spells come, you'll understand why, and you won't be tempted to cut the fund loose.

Further, you need to know what the portfolio looks like today because it can give you some idea about the fund's future risks. Remember, since these are new funds, you don't have historical risk measures, such as beta or standard deviation, to use as resources. Funds with bloated P/Es relative to their market-cap peers will probably carry higher betas and standard deviations than those funds with lower price ratios. Funds owning fewer stocks will generally be more volatile than those holding many. Finally, managers who concentrate in particular sectors will probably give you some volatility, too. You can find all this information on a fund's Fund Report.

We tend to look kindly on funds launched by respected shops, and we're generally optimistic about their chances. Keep in mind, though, that too much is never a good thing. Some fund companies send many similar offerings onto the field; this move draws media attention and it's a great way to reward up-and-coming portfolio managers. Still, it can also overwork a fund's analyst bench and backfire.

The name's not good enough

How Much Will It Cost?

When stocks are up 20% per year, costs might not seem important. After all, a 2% expense ratio off a 20% return leaves you with an 18% gain—and who would complain about that? But if your stock fund were to return, say, 8%, that 2% expense ratio leaves you with just a 6% gain. One-fourth of your return has just gone to cover expenses. Now that's a big deal. And regardless of the level of returns, paying more than you have to can cost you tens of thousands of dollars or more in compounded returns over time. So when evaluating rookie funds, be sure to consider their expense ratios.

You'll notice that new funds often carry higher expense ratios than older funds. That's often because small, new funds don't enjoy the same economies of scale that older, larger funds do: Larger funds have more shareholders to cover expenses. So when buying a rookie fund, you'll want to be sure that the fund's family has a history of bringing down costs as assets rise. You can determine a fund family's practice by examining the expense ratios of the family's more established funds. Expense ratios also appear on funds' Fund Reports.

Will This Fund Offer Any Extras?

You want your funds to be dedicated to you. Low costs are one way to express devotion, of course. But also favor rookies that vow to control their asset sizes by closing to new investors at particular asset points. As funds grow, managers can be forced to compromise their strategies to accommodate all that new money. But funds that close before becoming too large don't face that problem.

Look for managers who align their interests with yours by investing in their own funds. At Longleaf Partners, for example, fund managers can't own anything other than Longleaf Funds. Because these managers are shareholders, too, they are likely to keep costs lower and minimize taxable distributions.

New funds can certainly offer opportunity, but we recommend that you build your core around funds that have established track records and use rookies at the fringes of your portfolio. Consider investing a little in a rookie fund and dollar-cost averaging into it over time.

Fearless Facts

▶ Research the manager's previous record. Has he or she run a fund before? If so, what was the offering's record? If not, has the manager spent time on the bench of a successful fund?

▶ If the manager doesn't have much of a record, consider the fund company's historic performance. Consider how quickly a fund shop has adjusted or liquidated its stinkers, how long they've tolerated underperformance, and so on.

▶ Make sure the fund has a straightforward strategy that you understand. If the manager is a rookie, you probably don't want the fund shop to give him free rein.

▶ Stick with low costs. You've heard this before and you'll hear it again: Morningstar has found absolutely no correlation between expensive funds and successful funds.

▶ Some fund shops require that new managers commit their investment dollars to their own funds. That generally guarantees that the manager's interests are right in line with the shareholders'.

Quiz

1   Which rookie fund shouldn't you consider?

Answers to this quiz can be found on page 276

a   One run by a manager with a previous track record.

b   One run by a manager with no mutual fund experience.

c   One run by a manager with no mutual fund experience working for a reputable fund family with an established strategy.

2   Why is it important to examine a rookie fund's portfolio?

a   To set realistic expectations for the fund's performance.

b   To get a handle on the potential risks of the investment.

c   Both.

3   Why should you favor managers who invest in their own funds?

a   Their interests are aligned with yours.

b   They are better investors.

c   They have more experience.

4   Why do rookie funds often cost more than established funds?

a   Because rookie funds are investing in harder-to-research stocks.

b   Because rookie funds generally have fewer shareholders to cover costs.

c   Because all new funds are overpriced.

5   Rookie funds should:

a   Make up the core of your portfolio.

b   Be held in small quantities, at least at first.

c   Be bought in large quantities.

Worksheet

Have you invested in a brand-new fund? What drove you to make that purchase?

What are some of the main differences to bear in mind when evaluating a rookie fund and one with a longer track record?

Are there any added risks associated with investing in a rookie fund? Why or why not?

Lesson 312: Avoiding Portfolio Overlap

Success! You have determined your investment goals, figured out what you'll need to earn to reach them, and found investments that match those goals and your risk tolerance. Your portfolio is built, and you're ready to relax.

Not so fast.

Face it: Investing is a lifetime activity and you'll need to continue to monitor what you have created. Just as a parent never stops parenting, an investor never stops investing. So even after making all these decisions, you now face a more difficult—yes, more difficult—part of the process: monitoring your portfolio and learning how and when to make changes.

One of the very first problems you may face is the problem of portfolio overlap: You may have one or two individual stocks (such as behemoths General Electric or Microsoft), investment styles, or sectors overrepresented in your portfolio. After investing for a while, investors often find that though their funds come in different wrappers, many have similar content. In other words, these investors have too much of one thing. To gauge how much overlap your portfolio has, you can do some hefty calculations by hand, using shareholder reports. Alternatively, you can enter your portfolio in a tracking tool such as Morningstar.com's Portfolio Manager.

To gauge your portfolio overlap, answer the following questions about your portfolio.

Do You Favor One Investment Style over Another?

The Morningstar style box can be an investor's best friend when it comes to making sure that your portfolio is still diversified. Based on a fund's most recent portfolio, the style box will not only tell you whether your manager has gone whole hog into large-value stocks, but it can also lead you to funds that bear little resemblance to one another. After all, value funds don't act much like growth portfolios, and small-cap funds behave differently from large-cap offerings. In style-box lingo, opposite corners should attract. If you're too heavy in large value, try increasing your position in large-growth, small-value, or small-growth offerings.

Do You Have Too Much in One Stock?

Sometimes, two funds' portfolios may look slightly different, but you need to be aware of how much you own of any particular stock. For example, both fund managers may have made outsized commitments to computer giant Microsoft, increasing your issue-specific risk.

If you invested in only one or two funds, you could determine your portfolio overlap by scouring shareholder reports and punching numbers into a calculator. But if you own more than a few funds or if you want to see just how another fund might change your current portfolio mix, this process is cumbersome. The Morningstar.com Instant X-Ray tool offers an easy way to check for overlap.

Avoiding Overlap

Top-15 Holdings for Fidelity Magellan		Top-15 Holdings for Fidelity Growth & Income	
% Net Assets as of 6/30/04		% Net Assets as of 6/30/04	
❶ Citigroup	4.22	❹ Microsoft	4.03
❷ American International Group	3.71	❸ General Electric	3.89
❸ General Electric	3.33	❻ ExxonMobil	3.70
❹ Microsoft	3.20	❺ Pfizer	3.67
❺ Pfizer	2.74	SLM	3.44
Viacom B	2.68	Verizon Communications	2.80
❻ ExxonMobil	2.17	SBC Communications	2.68
Johnson & Johnson	1.84	❽ Wal-Mart Stores	2.36
Home Depot	1.81	Fannie Mae	2.26
❼ Bank of America	1.78	❶ Citigroup	2.23
Cisco Systems	1.74	❷ American International Group	2.15
Tyco International	1.71	UnitedHealth Group	1.77
ChevronTexaco	1.70	❼ Bank of America	1.68
Intel	1.67	BellSouth	1.56
❽ Wal-Mart Stores	1.60	Wells Fargo	1.52

Eight of the top-15 holdings are the same in these two funds.

The program examines each fund's top holdings and weights them according to how much you have invested in each fund. If you have included individual stocks in your portfolio, the program can easily consider them in the final balance as well. This is particularly important if you own a significant amount of your employer's stock in your 401(k) plan; you may find that your mutual funds also own that same stock. There's nothing wrong with holding some of your employer's stock, but you need to balance that investment with the rest of your portfolio.

The nature of the beast	Sector overlap is nearly unavoidable but sector concentration is not. Here's why: Diversified stock funds are just that—diversified. They will generally seek to reduce risk by spreading assets across a variety of industries or sectors of the market.

Do You Favor One or Two Sectors over Others?

Even if you find that you don't have a lot of overlap in individual stock names, you may still be overexposed to one or two sectors of the market.

As an example, let's take technology, a sector that has received a lot of attention in the new century. Technology has been a wonderful long-term return story (most of us remember that it seemed like the only story in the late 1990s), so mutual fund managers have often spent a lot of money shopping in this industry. One of the reasons that the market's volatility was so painful for some of us in the last four years was that investors were generally more exposed to this sector than they had realized.

Growth funds, in particular, usually carried large tech weightings with lofty prices and even loftier earnings expectations. The average large-growth fund kept far more of its assets in technology stocks—

37% as of mid-2000—than in any other sector of the market. (In comparison, the S&P 500 Index had about 30% of its assets in tech stocks at the time.) Mid- and small-growth funds held even more of their assets, about 40%, in tech names. Many investors with multiple growth funds owned a lot more technology stocks than they realized. More recently, exposures to this sector have declined slightly as managers have hoped to find the next big thing in other industries.

The technology example may be overused, but that's partly because it was especially egregious. Keep in mind that at any given time there is likely to be a sector that grows to prominence among growth or value funds. It's a good idea to X-Ray your portfolio regularly to make sure that it hasn't gotten too skewed one way or another.

Do You Own Too Many Large-Cap Funds?

Large-cap offerings make great core holdings, but it's easy to overdose on them. After all, they often get a lot of media coverage, they're easy to buy, and they're pretty simple to understand. It's vital that investors avoid large-cap addiction—especially large-cap offerings from the same fund family.

Here's why: The large-cap universe is relatively small. Less than 9% of all stocks can be classified as "large cap." Generally, a fund shop's managers will draw upon a single research pool, so there's a good chance of overlap if you buy multiple large-cap funds from a single family. Incidentally, the odds of duplication increase if you stick to large-blend funds, the universe of the S&P 500. In fact, there is little justification for owning more than one large-blend fund. So once you have picked up a large-value and a large-growth fund—or a single large-blend fund—start looking at options elsewhere in the style box.

Do You Own Multiple Funds Run by the Same Manager?

Zebras don't change their stripes, and fund managers rarely change their investment styles. If you own two funds managed by Famous Manager A, chances are you own two of the same thing. That's because managers generally have ingrained investment habits that they apply to every pool of money they run. So no matter how much you love a particular manager, don't buy more than one of his or her offerings if you are serious about diversification. Owners of Mutual Shares, formerly run by Michael Price, wouldn't have gained much from picking up sibling Mutual Beacon.

The (most) usual suspects	Portfolio overlap usually creeps up on investors. Here's a quick and dirty list of what to watch for.
	1. Too much exposure to just one investing style.
	2. Too much exposure to just one sector.
	3. Too much loyalty to one manager. You may love your portfolio manager, but it's unlikely that you need more than one of his or her funds.
	4. Too much loyalty to a (smaller) investment shop. Very few boutique shops can cover all of your investing needs.

Do You Own Multiple Funds from One Boutique Family?

The Matthews funds are specialists in Asia; Oakmark concentrates on value. Such fund families are excellent at what they do, but it's unlikely that owning three of their funds gives you much more than you'd get with one.

Nevertheless, many of the big firms provide opportunities to diversify, and a handful, such as Fidelity and Vanguard, can truly claim to be one-stop shops. Moreover, many savvy fund families now offer their own fund supermarkets, which allow investors to sample funds from other shops while still remaining loyal to their favorite families. That's a win-win situation.

Fearless Facts

 Know your habits. Portfolio overlap occurs when investors over-commit to one or more of the following:

- ► Investment styles
- ► Individual sectors
- ► Individual companies
- ► Large-cap funds
- ► One or two managers
- ► Just one small firm

 Morningstar's Instant X-Ray enables you to quickly size up whether your portfolio is overexposed to a certain investment style.

 If your large-cap blend fund is well-diversified, you probably just need one. Look to the small-growth or small-value categories to diversify.

Quiz

1   Why is portfolio overlap a greater risk for fund investors who also own individual stocks?

a	Because individual stocks are riskier than funds.
b	Because the investor's funds may also own this stock, making the investor's overall portfolio more concentrated than it seems.
c	Portfolio overlap isn't a greater risk for fund investors who also own individual stocks.

Answers to this quiz can be found on page 276

2   If you own a lot of growth funds, chances are you're overweight in what sector of the market?

a	Technology.
b	Financials.
c	Utilities.

3   How many large-blend funds should you own if you already have a large-value and a large-growth fund?

a	Two.
b	One.
c	Maybe none.

4   If you own one fund run by Manager A, how many other funds of his or hers should you own if you value diversification?

a	None.
b	One.
c	As many as you want.

continued...

5   If you own one fund from a boutique fund family, how many other funds should you own from that same family if you value diversification?

a	None.
b	One.
c	As many as you want.

Worksheet

Using the Instant X-Ray tool on Morningstar.com, take a look at your mutual fund portfolio. Are your funds well-diversified across the Morningstar style box or clustered in just a few squares? How do your portfolio's sector weightings compare with those of the S&P 500 Index?

Do you have more exposure to a certain investment style or sector than you would like? How can you adjust your portfolio to diversify your portfolio or decrease the risk you're taking?

What are the risks of investing in the same fund family or with the same fund manager?

What are the advantages and disadvantages of investing with a large fund family? A small boutique?

Know When to Sell Your Mutual Fund

Lesson 313: Fund Warning Signs

All good things must come to an end. We all know about the shelf-life of television shows, for example. Remember when *Who Wants to be a Millionaire?* was the most exciting thing happening to American audiences?

Mutual funds can also lose their magic. We'd love to say that a good fund will always be good, but funds change. Performance slips. Managers leave. Strategies evolve. That's why funds need to be monitored.

Here are some of the warning signs to watch out for. These aren't sell signals per se: Instead, think of these as signals that change may be on the way—the mutual fund equivalent of dwindling audiences, sour writing, and producer desperation.

Asset Growth

This may seem counterintuitive, but sometimes mutual funds actually need smaller audiences. As funds attract new investors and grow larger, their returns often become sluggish, weighed down by too many assets. They lose their potency and their returns revert to the average for their group. Some funds stop accepting money from new investors when their assets grow too large, but many don't. That explains why so many once-hot funds become mediocre.

There are worse things than being average, of course. But you may still want to keep an eye on your funds as they grow, especially your small-growth funds. Sometimes mutual fund shops will do the monitoring for you. Vanguard International Explorer is one such example. The fund has put up strong numbers in the past few years, buying small-company stocks in foreign markets. That performance drew lots of attention from investors, and the fund's asset base swelled. Vanguard tried to stem the tide of new money in the spring of 2004 by hiking the fund's minimum-investment amount, but investors weren't deterred. The shop was forced to close the fund to new investors over the summer.

Even shops known for their discipline and their great performance can get caught in this trap. American Century Ultra racked up excellent returns in the 1990s picking small firms with lots of growth potential. The management team was vigilant about selling companies as soon as their share prices increased. Investors flocked to the fund, but returns eventually slowed because the managers just couldn't execute their fast-trading, super-growth strategy with so many assets in tow. So what did they do? They changed their strategy. They now buy larger companies and trade less often.

American Century's strategy change is a perfect example of the second side effect of asset growth: Fund managers often have to alter their strategies to accommodate new money. Some simply buy more stocks, buy larger companies, or trade less. (When big funds trade frequently, they risk affecting their stocks' share prices as they buy and sell.) No matter what they do, though, they have to make concessions or close the fund. And as a shareholder, you need to be aware of the change and consider whether or not this altered fund fits into your portfolio. American Century Ultra shareholders no longer own a small-growth fund, they own a large-growth fund.

Some types of funds are more hurt by asset growth than others. We'll talk more about this topic in our next lesson.

Manager Changes

Most mutual funds are only as good as the people behind them: the fund managers. Managers decide what to buy, what to sell, and when to make these changes. Because the fund manager is the person who is most responsible for a fund's performance, many investors wonder if they should sell a fund when their manager leaves.

Unfortunately, there is no one right answer to this question. You'll need to consider a few factors. For example, you may have to pay taxes on your sold shares, if they appreciated. And what you give up in taxes may not be offset by future gains in a different fund. You'll also need to consider the record of the new manager—perhaps he or she has already worked on the fund? Perhaps the manager has racked up a solid record at another offering? Keep in mind: A new manager may do just as well as the old.

Further, management turnover won't make much difference when it comes to certain kinds of investing styles. Consider index funds.

Managers of index funds are not actively choosing stocks, they're simply mimicking a benchmark. Thus, manager changes at index funds are less important than manager changes at actively managed funds. Sometimes, it's clear that management turnover is a non-issue. Some fund shops—Fidelity and T. Rowe Price are two examples—have deep benches, strong analyst training programs, and extensive research support. These firms have historically had plenty of talented managers and analysts who can take over when a manager departs. Similarly, funds run by teams are often less affected by manager changes. If one team member leaves, there are often two or three other managers who will remain behind.

Of course, changes in management can be a crushing blow to funds run by a single fund manager who has proved to be an adept stock-picker or trader in markets in which there are a wide range of possible returns (such as small growth or emerging markets). Manager changes at good funds from families that aren't strong overall are bad news, too.

Fund-Family Growth, Mergers, or Acquisitions

Why should it matter to your fund's performance if the sponsoring fund family decides that it wants to add some new funds to its line-up? Or that it wants to be sold or become independent? It may not seem like much, but those things can distract managers from doing their jobs. After all, if your employer is growing rapidly or is on an acquisition binge, doesn't that affect how you do your core job?

Once-great funds may also stall or lose their focus when their families expand and launch new offerings. Furthermore, funds can be forced to fill a different role as its family grows. Take Oakmark Fund. This one-time small-value fund is now firmly entrenched in mid- to large-cap territory. Initially, that upward shift was intentional. Former manager Robert Sanborn decided in 1994 to favor larger companies, believing that they were more competitive. However, as Oakmark expanded, it launched two dedicated small-cap funds, Oakmark Small Cap I and Oakmark Small Cap II. Now, even if current Oakmark manager Bill Nygren wanted to focus on small caps, it's unlikely that the fund would become all small again. The family already has funds that fill that role and the shop can't afford redundancy.

One of the best ways to stay abreast of changes at your mutual fund is to use the EDGAR section of the SEC's Web site, at www.sec.gov/edgar.shtml.

Keep alert

Keeping Watch

How can you find out if your funds are on the verge of change?

First, keep tabs on your fund families using the public information available. Regularly visit their Web sites and look for news of growth plans, mergers, and new fund launches. Get access to information on funds in the pipeline in the EDGAR section of the SEC's Web site (sec.gov), where fund families must register their funds. Finally, always scan the marketing materials that jam your mailbox.

Next, turn your attention to third-party sources, including Morningstar, and learn what these groups have to say about your funds and your fund families. Firms such as Morningstar aren't in the business of selling their own funds, and they take their roles as industry watchdogs seriously. Check out our fund news, read our fund analyses, and see what other investors in your funds are saying on our conversation boards. Make sure to read what members of the financial media are saying, too.

Finally, check up on your funds each month to make sure that things are status quo. Have their assets grown rapidly? Are their managers still in place? Is there anything notable going on with the fund family?

If you find that changes may be afoot, ask questions. If you find that your fund family is launching a new fund that sounds a lot like the fund you already own, for example, ask how the funds will differ and if this will mean more work for your fund manager. Or if you're worried about asset size, find out if the family plans to close the fund any time soon.

Fearless Facts

▶ Asset growth, management changes, and fund shop mergers and restructurings are signals that change could be on the way. That change could affect you, the shareholder, so you'll need to be alert.

▶ Peruse the financial section of national newspapers. Many of these sources have reporters that cover the mutual fund industry.

▶ Use independent sources. Morningstar includes information about management changes and fund shop restructurings on its Web site and in its print products.

▶ Consult industry watchdog groups, such as the SEC's EDGAR site. Funds are required to file changes with the commission.

▶ Keep in mind that you can always call your fund company directly if you have a question.

Quiz

1 A fund's asset growth can lead to many problems. Which of the following is not typically one of them?

a	Sluggish returns.
b	Higher expenses.
c	A change in investment strategy.

Answers to this quiz can be found on page 277

2 As funds grow, how do managers often change their strategies?

a	They buy more stocks.
b	They buy smaller stocks.
c	They trade more.

3 A manager change is:

a	Always a sell signal.
b	A warning sign that change may be on the way.
c	No big deal for most funds.

4 Why is it important to monitor your fund families?

a	Because they're the ones choosing securities for you.
b	Because fund family growth can mean change for the fund you own.
c	All of the above.

5 Which is not a good way to find out if your fund is on the verge of change?

a	Keep an eye on your fund's performance only.
b	Regularly visit your fund company's Web site.
c	Read what Morningstar and other third-party sources have to say about your fund and fund family.

Worksheet

What are three signals that your mutual fund's performance may slow down or take a turn for the worse?

Do you own any closed funds? When did they close and why? Do you think the fund family closed the fund at the right time?

Do you own any open funds with large asset bases? Have you seen your fund's asset size hinder or change the manager's strategy?

Have any of your funds undergone management changes since you've owned them? If so, has your fund's performance or investment style changed since the new manager came aboard?

Lesson 314: Where and Why Asset Size Matters

Bigger is usually better. Most people would prefer a rambling villa to a studio apartment. And everyone remembers the popularity of the Super Size meal at McDonald's.

But as it turns out, the Super Size meal was a disaster for American health; McDonald's plans to discontinue it in 2004. And super sized mutual funds can be just as troublesome. As hot shot funds grow, their returns often become sluggish, weighed down by too many assets. They lose their potency and become average. It happened to Fidelity Magellan. Magellan is still a fine investment, but it's no longer the total-return powerhouse it was when it had less than a billion dollars under its belt.

Asset size can impede performance for any fund, but some types of funds are hurt more than others. It depends on a fund's style. (Note that bond funds don't typically struggle with asset growth. Individual corporate bonds may have less of an impact on performance as bond fund's assets grow, but in general the bond market is sufficiently large that asset growth doesn't hamper many bond fund managers.)

Asset Size and Market Cap

A fund's asset size is simply the total amount of dollars invested in the fund at a certain point in time; it is the fund's NAV multiplied by the number of shares outstanding. Most funds report their assets monthly; the net asset figures on Morningstar's Fund Reports are usually as of the most recent month end.

There's no direct relationship between a fund's size and the size of the companies in which it invests. A fund with a $10 billion asset base, for example, doesn't necessarily own large-cap companies with $10 billion market capitalizations. It can buy stocks of any size—theoretically, at least.

The bottom line	Be demanding in your search for fund companies that appear to have your best interests at heart. Morningstar has found that generally, the best fund companies tend to close when asset size becomes unwieldy. You can check a fund shop's record using the SEC's EDGAR site, but Morningstar's Fund Reports include the same information—for a lot less hassle!

We say "theoretically" because very large funds may have difficulty buying very small stocks. It's tough to put large dollar amounts to work in a small market. Small-cap stocks take up less than 10% of the U.S. market's overall assets; large caps, meanwhile, account for more than 80% of the market. In other words, in terms of number, large-cap stocks are a small part of the market (as you know, there just aren't an unlimited number of GE-size firms). In terms of market cap, though, they dominate. It's therefore easier for a fund manager with a lot of assets to buy bigger companies than to own a small fry.

Let's take an example. If Fidelity Magellan, with almost $65 billion in assets in mid-2004, was really bullish on sunglass-maker Oakley and wanted to make it a large part of its portfolio, it couldn't. The value of all of Oakley's shares combined is about $800 million; if Magellan could buy all of it—and legally it cannot—Oakley would still make up just 1% of the portfolio. A fund with fewer assets would have a much easier time loading up on Oakley's shares.

Asset Size and Turnover

It would seem that too many assets pose the biggest threat to small-company funds. But Morningstar's preliminary research—which examined the risk-adjusted performance of all types of funds—suggests that isn't necessarily the case. We've found that asset size is not a problem for all small-company funds. Instead, asset overload tends to threaten growth funds of all market capitalizations and is especially detrimental to small-cap growth funds that trade a lot.

Some Good Firms Have Seen Titanic Asset Growth

Fund Family	1999 Year-End Net Assets ($)	2003 Year-End Net Assets ($)	% Change
American Funds	326,685,736,512	450,851,436,489	38
Calamos	205,250,375	12,118,671,905	5804
Dodge & Cox	10,736,463,075	27,879,000,000*	160
Royce	1,941,184,299	8,837,687,788*	355
Wasatch	534,962,948	4,837,637,711	804

Data through January 31, 2004. *Third-Quarter-End Net Assets

In fact, trading seems to be the key. Value funds trade far less than growth funds and therefore incur lower trading costs. (The average growth fund's turnover rate is well over 100%, much higher than the average value fund's.)

When most people think of trading costs, they think only of brokerage commissions—less trading, lower costs. But there is a second component of trading costs: the cost of "moving the market." This is a component that is directly affected by asset size. Funds can "move" the market when they are unable to buy stocks without pushing the share price of that company upward as they're buying; likewise, funds that are "market movers" cannot sell stocks without pushing the price downward as they're selling.

Trading Volumes Can Challenge Funds

Fund Family	Turnover Rate %	Median Daily Trading Volume %	Girth Measure %
American Funds	31	1500	465
Calamos	60	55	33
Dodge & Cox	19	1371	260.49
Royce	40	1071	428.4
Wasatch	65	1042	677.3

Data through January 31, 2004.

Morningstar's "girth measure" attempts to capture the effects of asset bloat for certain fund families.

Think of the stock market as a giant auction house. In an auction, the price of an object goes up as more people bid for it. As more people enter the bidding, the price rises, making the object more expensive for the eventual purchaser. Now think of each dollar in a mutual fund as another bidder. The larger the fund, the more likely it will be to boost a firm's share price simply by "bidding" on its shares.

Growth and value funds are both affected by this phenomenon, but growth funds usually suffer more. That's because growth managers are usually competing with plenty of other buyers for popular merchandise—high-priced, high-growth stocks. They're like the people who go to auctions and bid on Jackie Onassis's jewelry. Value managers, on the other hand, are like shoppers combing through yard sales every weekend. Because there's a lot less competition for a beaten-up lawn chair with hidden potential than for Jackie's string of pearls, prices don't get "moved" nearly as much.

How Funds Can Manage Asset Growth

There are a few things funds can do to manage asset growth. First, they can close. Closed funds don't accept money from new investors, but they'll usually continue to take investments from current shareholders. Their asset bases may grow, but at a more moderate pace than when they were open. Some funds close to current investors, too, which means that even those who own the fund already can't contribute any more to it. But that's pretty rare.

More often than not, fund managers cope with huge asset bases by altering their strategies. Some will buy more stocks. Heartland Value, for example, held about 50 stocks when its asset base was in the hundred millions; when assets topped $2 billion in 1997, the fund owned more than 300 names. Other funds will start buying larger stocks, as American Century Ultra did. Still others will hold cash because they just can't find enough stocks to buy.

How You Can Handle Asset Growth

So what does all this mean for your portfolio? Well, you probably don't have to worry as much about your value funds getting too big. But keep an eye out for sluggish risk-adjusted performance from your fast-trading growth funds as their asset bases rise.

When choosing growth funds, you can tilt the odds in your favor a few ways. Favor funds and fund shops that vow to close at a particular asset size. Adventurous types often try jumping into hot growth funds and then jumping out once they gather too many assets. But be warned: That practice could just as easily lead to large losses as to great returns, and because of the selling that you'll inevitably have to do, it's not suitable for taxable accounts.

As assets grow, keep an eye out for strategy changes. If you bought a fund to fit a small-growth niche in your portfolio, you might not be happy if its median market cap creeps up. A fund with a big cash stake can throw off your own asset-allocation decisions. Even if a growing fund is thriving, asset growth may still mean problems.

Fearless Facts

▶ Be particularly wary of asset bloat when it comes to your growth funds.

▶ Check your smaller-cap fund's turnover rates. Offerings that trade often are usually the first to suffer due to asset growth. Rapid traders who manage growing funds can have a tough time putting money to work in the small-cap universe and performance can suffer.

▶ Remember to favor funds that are willing to close their doors when their asset bases expand.

▶ Be aware that many managers won't necessarily change their strategies when assets balloon. Instead, they'll sit on a pile of cash. That isn't necessarily a bad thing, but keep in mind that you're paying fees so that managers can invest in companies for you. If you wanted a money market fund, there are cheaper, easier ways to buy one!

Quiz

1 Why can very large funds have difficulty buying very small stocks?

a	Because it's tough to put large dollar amounts to work in a small stock.
b	Because the small-cap market is so big.
c	Because small-cap stocks are tough to research.

Answers to this quiz can be found on page 277

2 According to Morningstar research, which type of fund is most threatened by asset growth?

a	Value funds.
b	Low-turnover growth funds.
c	High-turnover small-growth funds.

3 Why do growth managers move the market more than value managers when they buy and sell stocks?

a	Because growth managers are buying securities other investors are also interested in.
b	Because growth managers are buying securities others investors aren't interested in.
c	Because growth managers trade less.

4 What is not something funds usually do to handle asset growth?

a	Close to new investors.
b	Alter their strategies.
c	Own fewer stocks.

continued...

5 If you're concerned about asset growth, what should you do?

a	Favor funds with low turnovers.
b	Buy aggressive, fast-trading funds.
c	Don't buy any growth funds.

Worksheet

Asset growth tends to affect small-cap funds more than large-cap offerings, and growth funds more than value-oriented funds (because growth funds tend to have higher turnover). Do you own any smaller-cap and/or high-turnover growth funds that could be vulnerable to asset bloat?

If so, has your fund company said anything about the asset level at which it might consider closing the fund?

Do you invest in any funds that have been forced to increase their average market capitalizations or number of holdings due to asset growth? Did you continue to invest in the funds? Why or why not?

Lesson 315: When to Sell a Fund

While most of us can agree on what to look for when buying a fund—good risk-adjusted returns, long manager tenure, etc.—we often part ways on when to sell. Just check out some of the long and lively debates raging on Morningstar's conversation boards.

None of us wants to be one of those investors who undermines his or her returns by buying and selling at the wrong times. Yet some situations almost demand that we hit the sell button.

The Fund Loses More than It Should

Suppose a bond fund loses more than 23% in a year in which its average peer suffers a much slimmer loss. That was the case with Merrill Lynch World Income in 1998, a multisector-bond fund that made a big bet on emerging-markets debt in general and Russian debt in particular. Shareholders who expected boring bond performance should have sold.

The Fund Gains More than It Should

This might sound illogical—after all, who complains about great returns? But if your "moderate" balanced fund posts a 60% return when its average peer is up 10%, maybe you don't own what you think you do.

The Fund Changes Its Strategy

Presumably, you buy a small-value fund because you want exposure to small-value stocks. If the manager suddenly starts buying large-growth stocks, you may have a problem. After all, you may already have a large-growth fund in your portfolio.

Be careful in how you define a change in style, though. Sometimes a manager's stocks and habits will change, even though his underlying strategy hasn't. Baron Asset is a case in point. The fund didn't migrate from the small-growth to the mid-cap growth category because manager Ron Baron began buying larger stocks. He still buys small-cap issues; he just holds onto them as they move into mid-cap or large-cap range.

The Fund Underperforms for a Long Period

While one year of underperformance may be nothing to worry about, two or three ugly years can get frustrating. The urge to sell intensifies.

Before pulling the trigger, be sure you're comparing your underperformer to an appropriate benchmark, such as its Morningstar category peers or a suitable index. Before you pass judgment, make sure the manager or strategy hasn't changed.

Your Goals Change

You don't invest to win some imaginary race, but to meet your financial goals. As your goals change, your funds should change as well.

Suppose you start investing in a balanced fund with the goal of buying a house within the next five years. If you get married and your spouse already owns a house, you may decide to use that money for retirement instead. In that case, you might ditch the balanced fund for a pure stock fund. Your goal and the time until you draw on your investment have changed.

Many fund companies have faced regulatory action alleging that they engaged in behavior that hurt their shareholders. These firms include some of the industry's biggest names, such as AIM Investments, Alger, Alliance Bernstein, Excelsior, Federated, Franklin, Heartland, ING Investments, Invesco, Janus, PGHG, PIMCO, Putnam, Scudder, RS, and Strong. Check their status early and often, using media sources or independent groups such as Morningstar. Morningstar's site has a current page (www.morningstar.com/fii/fundindustryinvestigations.html) that tracks the fund industry investigations.

Legal woes in 2004

They're in Trouble....Big Trouble.

The past year has been a tough one for the mutual fund industry. New York Attorney General Eliot Spitzer has filed numerous complaints referencing more than 20 big-time mutual fund shops, including the MFS, Janus, Putnam, and Scudder offerings.

Keep in mind that many of these shops are still under investigation and not all are guilty as charged. Others, meanwhile, have settled with regulators and instituted meaningful reforms. In general, though, this is a time to be vigilant about what's happening at your funds. Read the newspapers. Check with sources such as Morningstar. You need—and deserve—mutual fund companies that you can trust.

You Just Can't Take It Anymore

The point of investing is meeting financial goals, not developing ulcers. If your fund is so volatile that not even the vision of your brand new house calms you down, then by all means sell—as long as you'd never buy the fund or a fund like it again.

The moral: Know your funds, know yourself, and never make the same mistake twice.

Fearless Facts

 Remember: It was Kenny Rogers who said that you've gotta know when to hold 'em—and know when to fold 'em. Your sell discipline is as important as your buying decision.

 It's time to consider selling a fund if:

- The offering loses more than it should, given its investment strategy.
- The fund gains more than it should, considering its approach.
- The shop announces a change in strategy. This offering may no longer be able to play the same role in your portfolio.
- The fund lags its category and its benchmark for a prolonged period (more than three years).
- You no longer need the fund because your goals have changed.
- The fund company is in legal trouble. If a fund shop plays fast and loose with the SEC's rules, the shop doesn't have the shareholders' best interests at heart. Period.
- A fund's risk is too much to handle.

Quiz

1 What is not a good reason to consider selling a fund?

a	It loses more than it should.
b	It gains more than it should.
c	It performs just as you expected.

Answers to this quiz can be found on page 278

2 Style shift:

a	Always indicates a change in strategy.
b	Sometimes indicates a change in strategy.
c	Is always a sell sign.

3 Before cutting an underperforming fund, check its:

a	One-year return against the market.
b	One-year return against its peers.
c	Three-year return against an appropriate index and its peers.

4 If you began investing for retirement and now your goal is to buy a home in two years:

a	You may need to sell some of your aggressive funds.
b	You may need to sell some of your conservative funds.
c	You shouldn't do a thing.

5 Is it okay to sell a fund that you've lost money on?

a	No.
b	Yes.
c	Maybe.

Worksheet

Have you ever sold a mutual fund before? Do you remember why you made that decision? Did you decide to sell because of a change in the fund's fundamentals (a management or strategy change, for example), because of poor performance, or because your own goals and risk tolerance changed?

Most mutual fund managers have a so-called "sell discipline"—catalysts that will prompt them to sell their holdings. Look down the list of mutual funds that you own. What factors or events would prompt you to sell each of your holdings?

Do you have any "lemons" in your portfolio? Is it time to sell? How do you know?

Lesson 316: Rebalancing Your Portfolio

So you've built a portfolio that perfectly matches your needs. If only you could kick back and ignore it until retirement. In order to keep your portfolio in shape, you have to monitor it on a regular basis. You'll want to reevaluate all of your funds and make sure that you don't have a reason to sell any of them. You'll also want to make sure that your asset allocation hasn't become lopsided—and if it has, you'll want to rebalance your holdings.

In this lesson, we'll examine why rebalancing matters and offer our suggestions for how and when you should rebalance your portfolio.

Why Rebalance?

Say that you originally constructed a portfolio of 60% stocks, 30% bonds, and 10% cash. If left alone over a 20-year period, that portfolio could easily morph into a blend of 84% stocks, 13% bonds, and 3% cash. Presumably, you set up your original allocation to match your needs and your risk tolerance. If neither has changed, your allocation shouldn't either. For example, if stocks take over your portfolio (as they did in our example), your returns may rise but so will your risk. Moreover, you may find yourself with insufficient cash on hand to meet short-term needs. The only way to return the portfolio to the original risk level is by buying and selling funds until you reach your original allocation. That's what rebalancing is.

Our Rebalancing Principles

If you ever watched *The Ed Sullivan Show*, you probably remember the plate-spinning act—the guy who kept all that fine china spinning precariously atop long, flexible rods. It was pretty impressive, all those place settings gyrating at once as the performer ran back and forth to give each rod a flick and keep it all from toppling down.

If you were to rebalance your portfolio frequently, you'd feel a lot like this guy. Relax. Rebalancing your portfolio doesn't have to be a juggling act if you follow our guidelines.

Don't rebalance too often. You needn't worry about rebalancing every quarter, or even every year. Morningstar has found that investors who rebalanced their investments at 18-month intervals reaped many of the same benefits as those who rebalanced more often. Moreover, investors who rebalance less frequently save themselves unnecessary labor and, in the case of taxable investments, a good bit of money. That's because rebalancing requires paring back the winners, which means realizing capital gains and, for the taxable investor, paying Uncle Sam. We're not saying you should only look at your portfolio every 18 months—in fact, we think you should monitor your portfolio regularly to watch out for manager or strategy changes at your individual funds. But resist the urge to tinker unless one of your funds has significantly changed its strategy.

If you rebalance just one thing, make it the stock/bond split. Your cash and bond stakes are vital to keeping your portfolio's risk in check. Because bonds don't generally move in sync with your stock investments, a simple strategy of restoring your cash and bond funds to their original weightings every 18 months will dramatically lower your portfolio's overall risk.

Rebalancing forces investors to buy low and sell high—one of the hardest thing to do when it comes to participating in the markets. If you do nothing else, try to keep your stock and bond portfolio balanced. Choose an allocation that fits your risk profile and check in on it every 18 months.	**Rule of thumb**

Rebalance subasset classes and investment styles by the numbers. Like any good concept, rebalancing can be taken to extremes. Some investors follow very detailed asset allocations that involve, say, putting 20% of their portfolio in large-growth funds and 15% in small-value funds. They then rebalance when the large-growth/small-value allocation gets out of whack, as well as when their overall stock/bond/cash allocation goes awry. That stock/bond/cash allocation clearly should be your rebalancing priority, as we've pointed out. When it comes to subasset classes or investment styles, we've found that readjusting whenever one style takes up one-fourth more or less than its original portfolio position can be an effective straegy. For example, you'd want to rebalance when the fund to which you devoted 20% of your portfolio rises to 25% or sinks to 15%.

Use new money to restore balance. Taxable investors take note: When adding fresh dollars to your portfolio, add to your laggards to avoid the tax consequences of selling your winners. If you don't have new money to put to work, consider having your funds' income and capital-gains distributions paid into a money market account, then using that cash for rebalancing.

Fearless Facts

▶ Remember: Reevaluate your portfolio's balance every 18 months.

▶ Your first rebalancing priority is always the portfolio's stock/bond mix. Choose a balance that's appropriate for your stage in life and investment goals. Stick with it.

▶ When it comes to the details (small growth versus large value and so on), rebalance only when an asset class grows or shrinks beyond 25% of its original position.

▶ The best way to rebalance is to use new money. If your large-value stake has grown from 16% to 22% of the portfolio, it's time to rebalance. But selling off that entire increase could mean a heavy tax burden. Instead, put new dollars to work in your portfolio's lagging asset groups.

Quiz

1   What is rebalancing?

Answers to this quiz can be found on page 278

   a   Restoring your portfolio to its original risk level by buying and selling funds until you reach your original allocation.

   b   Putting together a portfolio of mutual funds.

   c   Allowing stocks to take up more of your portfolio.

2   How often does Morningstar suggest that you rebalance your portfolio?

   a   Every quarter.

   b   Every year.

   c   Every 18 months.

3   Which is the most important part of your portfolio to rebalance?

   a   Your individual fund holdings.

   b   Your subasset-class or investment-style breakdown.

   c   Your asset allocation of stocks, bonds, and cash.

4   Morningstar suggests that you should rebalance your subasset classes/ investment styles how often?

   a   Whenever one subasset class or investment style takes up 25% more or less than its original portfolio position.

   b   Every year.

   c   Every 18 months.

5   Which way is not a way to restore balance to your portfolio?

   a   Add new money to your laggards.

   b   Add new money to your leaders.

   c   Use cash from your funds' income and capital-gains distributions.

Worksheet

How often do you rebalance your portfolio? How do you decide when to rebalance?

Let's say you had a portfolio that held 70% stocks, 25% bonds, and 5% cash. If you did not touch this portfolio for 15 years, would you expect the asset class weightings to change? Why or why not?

What sort of problems could arise from rebalancing too often?

How might your investment goals be related to rebalancing your portfolio?

If your portfolio is in a taxable account, how can you use new money to rebalance your portfolio and avoid Uncle Sam (to some degree)?

Lesson 317: Calculating Your Personal Rate of Return

Your fund says it finished the year up 15%. The Morningstar Fund Analyst Report says the same. Yet you only made 10% on the fund for the year.

The fact is, returns depend a lot on how you calculate them. Your actual investment or personal rate of return in a fund may be better—or worse—than you think. Knowing your portfolio's actual returns can help you determine if you're on track to meet your investment goals, and whether your funds are living up to your expectations.

Reported Returns vs. Personal Rate of Return

The simplest way to calculate return numbers—and the way Morningstar and most other sources do it—is to assume you made a single lump-sum investment at the beginning of the reporting period. So the 15% return on your fund assumes that you bought all of your shares right at the beginning of the year.

Often, however, your personal rate of return will be different. If you bought or sold shares during the period for which a return is being calculated, or if you didn't buy exactly at the period's start, your personal return won't match the formulaic return. Put another way: Your fund's trailing 12-month return doesn't tell you how you've been doing if you invested $100 each month rather than $1,200 up front.

Calculating Your Personal Return

Even though personal rates of return are crucial numbers for any investor trying to reach a goal, few fund families provide these returns on investors' account statements. Why not? Many fund companies brush off any suggestions for improved disclosure by arguing that providing more information would only confuse investors, or by pointing to surveys showing that shareholders are satisfied with the status quo.

Why you should care	Your personal return often offers a clue to your investing psyche. For example, if the fund reports a miserable year (it dropped into the red after an impressive first-quarter run and never got out), while your personal return is solid, it may be that your sell urge is spot-on (perhaps you thought those first-quarter returns were unsustainable). Personal returns can also highlight our bad habits, such as chasing hot returns or selling too late.

Until things change, you're on your own when it comes to calculating your personal rate of return. If you choose to enter a Transaction Portfolio in our Portfolio Manager, you can determine your personal gain or loss in individual funds (and in your entire portfolio) since you made an investment. Or you can enter the dates and prices of any purchases or sales into a financial calculator, or use the internal-rate-of-return function included in spreadsheet software.

How to Do It

Here's what you need to calculate personal returns for a single year:

► Your ending balance from the preceding year (for a single fund or for a portfolio of funds). For the sake of our example, let's say the preceding year's balance is $2,500.

► Your ending balance from the year for which you're calculating the returns. In our example, we'll use a final balance of $5,250.

► How much you invested during the year and the months in which you made the investments. In our example, the investments were $1,000 in May and $1,500 in November.

Note that the beginning balance and the investments during the year are negative numbers when you're using a financial calculator or spreadsheet. That's because you're trying to figure out the internal return represented by the difference between the $5,250 you ended up with and the $5,000 you invested ($2,500 beginning balance plus two investments during the year of $1,000 and $1,500).

If you're using a financial calculator, here's what to do:

1. Make a chart of your monthly cash flows. For a portfolio, pool together the cash flows for all of your funds. Assume that all investments during a month are made at the beginning of that month. Sum your initial balance and any January investment for the first month's entry. Also, determine the value of your fund at the end of the holding period. Locate the cash-flow function on your financial calculator and clear the memory of any old data.

2. As your calculator prompts you, enter cash flows. (Inflows are negative and outflows are positive.) Enter 0 for months with no cash flows and enter your ending balance as the final, positive cash flow.

3. Choose the IRR (internal rate of return—another term for personal rate of return) function on your calculator and compute. The result is your monthly personal rate of return.

4. To annualize your monthly IRR, follow these five steps:
(1) Divide your monthly IRR by 100. (2) Add 1. (3) Raise the number to the 12th power (12 months in a year). (4) Subtract 1. (5) Multiply by 100 to get the annual percentage.

What Personal Returns Tell You

Calculating your personal rate of return may not be your top choice for filling your free time on a Saturday afternoon. But doing so not only tells you how you're progressing toward your goals, but it also sheds some light on how well you've been investing.

If your personal returns are significantly lower than those listed in other sources or those reported by the fund company, take a close look at when you've been buying and selling. Maybe you bought hot funds after they had already hit the top, or sold when a fund was bottoming out and therefore missed a subsequent rebound. In that case, a disciplined dollar-cost-averaging program could keep you from sabotaging your results. You'll likely find that making short-term swaps in and out of the market—or between different funds—has hurt you more than it has helped.

Fearless Facts

▶ Personal returns are a good way to gauge your investing behavior. Your investing decisions usually show up in the difference between the fund's published return and your personal return.

▶ Use an Excel spreadsheet or invest in a business calculator in order to keep a handle on your personal rate of return. It'll save you numerous headaches as you get more involved in investing.

▶ Many 401(k) administrators will calculate your own individual rate of return for you.

Quiz

1   Why might your personal returns in a fund not match the fund's reported returns?

   a   Fund companies don't take sales costs into account when reporting returns.

   b   You didn't invest in the fund at the start of the period that the reported returns cover.

   c   All of the above.

Answers to this quiz can be found on page 279

2   Why does your personal rate of return matter?

   a   Because it's probably lower than you think.

   b   Because it's probably higher than you think.

   c   Because it helps you to evaluate how your portfolio and individual funds are performing.

3   Where can you always find your personal rate of return for a fund?

   a   Your account statement.

   b   The shareholder report.

   c   Neither.

4   When calculating your personal returns on a spreadsheet or financial calculator, why do you have to enter negative numbers for your contributions?

   a   You don't; you enter positive numbers.

   b   Because you're capturing the fact that assets are leaving your checking or savings account and going into a mutual fund.

   c   Because until you redeem your fund shares, those investments don't have real value.

continued...

5 If your personal rate of return for a fund is significantly lower than the reported return over the same period:

a	You're falling short of your goals.
b	You've probably miscalculated your personal return.
c	You may be buying and selling at inopportune times.

Worksheet

Perform an internal return rate (IRR) analysis on your fund portfolio. Is this value higher or lower than you expected?

How does your IRR compare with the returns printed in your fund's shareholder report or on a Morningstar Fund Report?

Why do you think your IRR is different from the reported return? What does this tell you about your timing in buying and selling funds?

What are the benefits of dollar-cost averaging?

Lesson 318: Calculating Your Cost Basis

Leave it to the IRS to complicate things.

The agency has pages and pages of tax laws and more forms than you can shake a stick at. It even has four ways of calculating something as simple as cost basis, or the price you paid for a security, including commissions and other expenses. Cost basis is important because you determine your profit (or loss) when you sell shares by subtracting your cost basis from the shares' current selling price. That difference is the amount the government taxes.

Cost basis may seem pretty straightforward—and it is, if you buy a security only at one point in time. But what if you've been investing a little bit in a fund over a period of years? That's when things get tricky. Choose one method for cost basis over the others and you may be able to keep more for yourself and give less to Uncle Sam.

First in, First Out (FIFO)

The most basic method for figuring cost basis is FIFO, or first in, first out. This approach assumes that, as you sell shares of a stock or mutual fund, you do so in the order in which the shares were purchased. While pretty straightforward, this procedure often leads to substantial taxable gains because the longer you hold shares in a rising market, the more they're worth. No wonder the IRS assumes you are using this method unless you indicate otherwise.

Specific-Share Identification

Specific-share identification, the second way to calculate cost basis, is for meticulous investors only. If you've kept careful records of when you bought stock or fund shares and how much you paid for them, you can ask a mutual fund or broker to sell specific shares. Normally, these shares would be the ones you paid the most for, since they would generate the smallest taxable gains.

But there's a catch. Gains are taxed at different rates depending on how long you've held the shares. Profits made on shares you've held for a year or less are taxed at rates significantly higher than those levied on shares held longer than a year. So consider the matter carefully before deciding to hawk expensive newer shares.

In short...	The real point of calculating your cost basis is to figure out what kind of tax liability you'll be facing down the road.

Single-Category Averaging

Another method for mutual fund investors is single-category averaging. Divide the total cost you paid for your shares by the total number of shares you own and voila, you have your average-cost basis for each share. Single-category averaging is quite popular with investors because it doesn't take much energy to calculate. But once you begin using it to compute cost basis, the IRS prohibits switching to another method without prior approval.

Double-Category Averaging

Finally, there's double-category averaging. Mutual fund shares are divided into short-term and long-term gains and are then averaged for cost basis. Of course, different tax rates apply to each category, and you must tell your mutual fund in writing how many shares from each category you want to sell. Definitely not a process for the faint of heart.

What's the Difference?

Which method works best varies from situation to situation.

Let's take an example. Robert bought 25 shares of the no-load Raging Bull Fund at $9 each in 1998. He purchased another 50 shares at $10 each in 2000, and 25 shares at $11 each in 2002. In early 2003, he decided to sell 30 of his 100 shares at $12 each, for a total sale of $360. Assuming all his gains are long term, which method for calculating cost basis should he use, and what will his taxable gains be?

If Robert uses FIFO, he'd sell his oldest shares first.

(25 ⊗ $9) ⊕ (5 ⊗ $10) ⊖ $275 cost basis

His taxable gains would be his total sale minus his cost basis.

$360 ⊖ $275 ⊖ $85

If Robert chooses the specific-shares method, he'd sell his most expensive shares first.

(25 ⊗ $11) ⊕ (5 ⊗ $10) ⊖ $325 cost basis

His taxable gains would be:

$360 ⊖ $325 ⊖ $35

If Robert goes the single-category averaging route, he'd divide the total cost of shares by the total number of shares owned to get his average share price. He'd then multiple by number of shares sold for total cost basis.

(25 ⊗ $9) ⊕ (50 ⊗ $10) ⊕ (25 ⊗ $11)

His taxable gains would be:

$360 ⊖ $300 ⊖ $60

Robert can't use the double-category averaging method because all his gains are long term.

Robert minimizes his taxable gains by using the specific-shares method: His taxable gains are just $35 versus $85 under FIFO and $60 using the single-category averaging method. With a little effort and a calculator, you can reduce Uncle Sam's take, too.

Fearless Facts

 In terms of your take-home return, taxes can be as important as expenses.

In a rising market, FIFO-style accounting can often take the biggest bite out of your aftertax return. However, it's also a quick and easy approach, one that you likely won't need help with.

Be aware: The IRS assumes that you use FIFO for all stock sales, unless you state otherwise!

Quiz

1 What is cost basis?

Answers to this quiz can be found on page 279

a	The amount you pay the IRS when you sell shares.
b	The price you paid for a security.
c	Your fund's annual costs.

2 To determine your profit or loss in a fund:

a	Subtract the cost basis from the current selling price.
b	Subtract the current selling price from the cost basis.
c	Add together the cost basis and the current selling price.

3 Which method for calculating cost basis is best?

a	FIFO.
b	Specific shares.
c	It depends on the situation.

4 In the single-category averaging method:

a	You sell the first shares you bought.
b	You divide the total cost you paid for your shares by the total number of shares you own and get an average-cost basis for each share.
c	You ask the fund to sell shares you paid the most for but have held for at least one year.

5 The double-category averaging method is only applicable if:

a	You have both short- and long-term gains.
b	You made a lump-sum investment and haven't added to it since.
c	You want to sell your entire position in the fund.

Worksheet

What are the advantages and disadvantages of each method of calculating your cost basis in a fund?

Why should you calculate cost basis? What does it tell you?

Think back to times when you sold shares in a fund. Would calculating the cost basis have helped make a decision as to which shares to sell? Could it have saved you money in the end?

Lesson 319: Is Your Retirement Portfolio on Track?

You will not work a day beyond your 55th birthday. And you plan to spend your retirement days sipping lemonade on Capri and stiffening your neck by watching two weeks of tennis at Wimbledon. You have no intention of being a stay-at-home retiree.

You might not have much choice, though.

Most likely, Social Security and your pension or retirement plan will only partially subsidize your dreams. According to 2002 government estimates, Social Security replaces about 40% of the average worker's preretirement earnings and that percentage may fall even lower in the future. Pensions or employer-sponsored retirement plans don't always cover the rest. Your own savings will more than likely make the difference between a retirement of jet-setting and one of sweater knitting.

So, in addition to monitoring your retirement portfolio and rebalancing as necessary, you should also calculate whether that portfolio is returning what it needs to be returning for your dream retirement. Here's how to do just that.

What Will Your Income Be?

The first step is determining what your regular retirement income will be, excluding your income from your own savings.

Request a Personal Earnings and Benefit Estimate Statement from the Social Security Administration (call 800-772-1213 or visit www.ssa.gov) to find out what you can expect each month from Social Security. Some people already receive this yearly, but if you haven't seen it yet, submit the form (which you can download or request over the phone), and the Social Security Administration will send you a list of estimated benefits, including your monthly retirement check in today's dollars. (Remember that Social Security benefits rise with inflation.)

If your Social Security benefits seem too skimpy, they may be. Not reporting name changes, using a name other than the one on your Social Security card, or entering an incorrect Social Security number can lead to inaccurate benefits calculations. Troubleshoot by checking your benefits every few years.

Projecting what your retirement or pension plan will provide requires more legwork.

First, know the reasons behind your expected future payments. Defined-benefit plans, such as a pension, often are linked to Social Security payments; consequently, a fatter Social Security benefit could mean a slimmer pension check.

Second, be persistent about seeking information. Some plans will update you regularly about your benefits as you near retirement. Others aren't as accommodating. Pester your employer's human-resources department for more information. If you get the run-around, turn to Washington. Call the Pension and Welfare Benefits Administration (800-998-7542) to find the Department of Labor office in your area. You can also ask for the free pamphlet "Protect Your Pension."

Pension and Welfare Benefits Administration, 800-998-7542
Social Security Administration (www.ssa.gov), 800-772-1213

Important numbers

Finally, don't overlook those pensions owed you from brief employment stints or from companies that have merged out of existence or gone belly up. Check the Pension Search Directory to discover whether you're one of the thousands of people who haven't claimed forgotten pensions.

How Much More You'll Need

Compare your expected pension and Social Security income with the amount of income you think you'll need. Determine whether or not your current investments will cover the difference between the two figures. Remember that you probably won't need the entire lump sum of your retirement costs the minute you retire. More than likely, your investments will continue to grow during your retirement. Premium subscribers can get help developing a full retirement plan with Morningstar.com's Retirement Planner tool.

Many Web-based programs demand a major assumption: the return you expect from your investments. Those with stock-heavy portfolios may be eager to plug in 13%—what the S&P 500 returned, with dividends reinvested, from 1982 to 2002—but that figure might not be accurate.

Since 1926, large-company stocks typically have returned a more sedate 11% per year, according to Ibbotson Associates' Stocks, Bonds, Bills, and Inflation. Investors retiring in 10 years or sooner should assume an even lower return—more like 8% per year. It's always better to use conservative projections and be surprised on the upside.

Intermediate-term bonds returned 5.3% per year, on average, between 1926 and 1997, a fair return to use for your bond positions. For cash, use the 3.8% average return of Treasury bills.

Making It All Add Up

If your current portfolio isn't generating the type of return you'll need for your retirement, consider the following:

Rethink your retirement lifestyle. Separate your needs from your wants. One way to save big: Lower your housing costs. Moving from a $300,000 home to a $200,000 home not only means more cash in your pocket but probably lower upkeep expenses, too.

If retirement is far enough away, get more aggressive. Trade some of your bond funds for conservative equity funds, or swap high-dividend stock funds for growth types.

Put off retirement, or work part-time. As of 2000, people of full retirement age (65 and 2 months) can receive their full Social Security benefits, no matter what their earnings are. Even if you begin receiving Social Security before reaching full retirement age, you can earn up to a certain amount and still receive full benefits.

Save more now so you can spend more later. This is hard. It's also common sense. Americans have shockingly low savings rates, shockingly high debt, and an alarming tendency to overspend.

Don't forget to reevaluate your situation every three to five years.

Fearless Facts

▶ Track down your Personal Earnings and Benefit Estimate Statement from the Social Security Administration in order to get a sense of what you can expect come the golden years.

▶ Estimate what you expected to receive and compare it with the statement; be vigilant about searching for errors. After all, the SSA has a client base of millions—literally—so you'll need to be your own advocate.

▶ Consult a financial advisor or an independent Web site or publication, such as Morningstar, to help you assess your needs for your retirement. Consider these in relation to what you can expect from Social Security and your savings plans.

▶ If you're not well-positioned for retirement, it's time to get going. Consider working a few more years, paring back your expectations, or—if you have time—introduce a slightly more aggressive tilt to a portion of your portfolio.

Quiz

1   What should be the components of your retirement nest egg?

Answers to this quiz can be found on page 280

   a   Social Security and pensions or employer-sponsored retirement plans.

   b   Social Security and personal savings.

   c   Social Security, pensions or employer-sponsored retirement plans, and personal savings.

2   How often should you reevaluate whether your portfolio is on track to meet your retirement needs?

   a   Every quarter.

   b   Every 18 months.

   c   Every few years.

3   When calculating expected returns for stocks, what number does Morningstar recommend that most investors use?

   a   18% per year.

   b   8% per year.

   c   4% per year.

4   What's a fair figure to use as an expected return for bonds?

   a   11% per year.

   b   5% per year.

   c   4% per year.

continued...

5   If you find that your portfolio is not on track and you plan to retire in just
    two years, which should not be an option?

a	Tweaking your portfolio so that it's more aggressive.
b	Rethinking your retirement lifestyle.
c	Saving more.

Worksheet

How much do you expect to spend each month when you're retired? To receive in benefits? How are your investments shaping up to fill that gap? (You can probably assume an 8% return from stocks, about 5% from bonds, and 3.8% from Treasury bills.)

Are there any adjustments you could make to your retirement plan to help reach your savings target? Could you save more, for example?

If retirement is a while away (more than 10 years), you might also consider shifting more of your portfolio into stock funds. What are the advantages and risks associated with such a move?

Investors typically shift from aggressively positioned stock funds (e.g., high-octane small- and mid-cap growth offerings) into more conservatively positioned vehicles (e.g., equity-income funds) as retirement draws near. Of the funds in your portfolio, which would you envision cutting back on as retirement approaches? Which might you add to?

Lesson 320: Refining Your Portfolio

You've turned out to be the model mutual fund investor. You monitor your portfolio regularly and have set up a rebalancing program. Every few years, you make sure your portfolio is on track to meet your goals. And you tweak things here and there when necessary.

This lesson involves dealing with change—specifically, how you may change over your investment lifetime. A life event, such as a death, birth, or marriage, may alter your investment approach. Tax entanglements or estate-planning dilemmas may lead you to seek the advice of a financial professional. Or you may simply find that you're itching to move beyond mutual funds and try your hand at stock investing. Here's how to handle each of those possibilities.

Entering a New Life Stage

Not every life event means change for every investor's portfolio. But we all should re-evaluate investment goals and risk levels after we pass into a new life stage.

For example, there's marriage. The dream of sharing your life with another person has become a reality. You then fantasize about buying a home together and about spending your golden years in side-by-side rockers. But those rockers will cost you. So will that home. You and your spouse need an investment plan that takes both of you into account. If you thought that planning for one person was tough, imagine planning for two.

Perhaps you've finally gotten a handle on that investing-for-two idea and, lo and behold, there are three—or more—of you. Saving for college turns into an obsession before the kid can even crawl. Then you feel the need to strike a better balance between work and motherhood. And before you know it, your daughter asks for $50 to go to the mall.

Suddenly, you're retired. Now you need an effective strategy for drawing on your portfolio while making sure it lasts as long as you do. And you want to leave something to your children while minimizing the tax burden.

In any of these examples, you need to step back to get your arms around your altered financial situation. Re-examine your money needs and goals, and readjust your investments accordingly.

Seeking Financial Advice

Maybe your nest egg becomes larger than you're comfortable managing on your own. Or you need estate-planning advice. Or you could use some tax help.

Even do-it-yourselfers sometimes find the need to work with a financial professional. To choose an advisor who suits your financial needs and personality, follow these four steps.

Decide what you want. Are you looking for someone to handle one part of your financial life, such as taxes or estate planning, or are you seeking a financial advisor who can take care of it all? Knowing the answer to that question helps you narrow your search to those advisors with skills to match your needs.

Once you've set your priorities, begin your search by asking your accountant or attorney for recommendations. Query friends and professional colleagues who work with advisors. Identify a handful of advisors whose services meet your needs, and then call to determine how much money you'll need to become a client. Confirm their services and specialties. After you've found a few good matches, schedule initial meetings, which should be free of charge.

Ask the right questions. Bring to that first meeting a checklist of questions, concerns, or issues you want addressed. Ask for and scrutinize a copy of the advisor's resume, known as the ADV form, as soon as you walk in the door. ADV forms include advisors' educational backgrounds and list which professional designations they hold. In Schedule F of the form, you'll discover how advisors are compensated, and whether they have business ties to particular insurance or mutual fund companies. If these ties exist, they should be disclosed to you in writing.

If you'll be relying on the advisor for investment suggestions—which funds or stocks to buy—be sure the two of you share the same investment philosophy. Ask advisors to walk you through their investment process, and to explain thoroughly what would make them sell a stock or fund. Request a copy of a typical financial plan.

Calculate the cost. Don't leave an advisor's office until you completely understand what the advice will cost—and get those details in writing. Have the advisor estimate what it will cost to create your plan and manage your investments, including both fees and commissions.

Conduct a background check. Ask the advisor for references from investment professionals (such as certified public accountants or certified financial planners) or attorneys who have seen the advisor's work before. Such professionals have reputations they won't want to jeopardize.

Rules of thumb	There are plenty of financial advisors out there, hungry for clients. We think the best thing you can do for yourself is research, research, research.

Next, contact professional and government regulatory organizations to verify that no disciplinary action has been taken against your candidate. Some resources are the CFP Board of Standards, the National Association of Securities Dealers, and the Securities and Exchange Commission.

Adding Stocks

After assembling and monitoring your portfolio of mutual funds, you may make a discovery: You like this investing stuff. Maybe you want to be your own fund manager—maybe you want to start investing in individual stocks.

In fact, investing isn't an either-or process; you don't need to be either a fund investor or a stock investor. You can be both.

Once you've developed your portfolio's core, feel free to break out of mutual funds and dabble in stocks. Stocks can do wonders for your portfolio. Of course, they can rev up returns. But they can also be great tax-management tools. Mutual funds can cause tax headaches. But stock investors get to decide when they take gains (or losses), and thereby determine their own tax destinies. You could, for example, defer gains if you choose, or sell a losing position to offset distributed gains in your funds.

If you decide to try your hand at stocks, where do you begin? Here are some of the key factors to consider. (This information is available in Morningstar's Stock Reports.)

Growth. Look for companies that are able to increase the size of their businesses consistently over time. In particular, look at how fast sales have grown relative to other companies in the same sector. Take into account the trend in sales growth—whether it's speeding up or slowing down—and its consistency during the past five years.

Profitability. Favor companies that earn consistently high returns on the money entrusted to them by shareholders. Examine the absolute value of a company's return on assets (ROA), a key measure of how well a company uses investors' money. Also look at the trend in those ROA ratios and their consistency.

Financial Health. Companies that keep debt low and generate cash every year could be worthy of your attention. Assess the strength of a company's balance sheet and the level of its free-cash flows.

Valuation. Size up a stock's price relative to others in its industry and the broad market.

Economic Moat. What are the company's competitive advantages? Could similar companies readily steal market share?

Fearless Facts

▶ Articulate to a potential advisor what kind of performance is important to you. You'll have to use fairly broad parameters, but it's possible to tell an advisor that you don't want to lose more than a certain percentage each year. A firm hand up front will ensure that you aren't exposed to risky investments.

▶ Ask a potential advisor what kinds of clients he or she has. Has he or she seen people with similar challenges? Experience counts. Remember, you can always ask to speak with a few of your potential advisor's clients.

▶ A rule of thumb is that the average rate for financial advice is about 1% for the first $1 million under management. This won't include the fees associated with mutual funds, however. If you're looking at flat fees, the advisor will probably charge you for the number of hours worked.

▶ Seek proof that your potential advisor is a Certified Financial Planner (CFP). If you're interested in tax help, look for someone who is also a Certified Public Accountant (CPA) or an Enrolled Agent. You can also be confident about someone who is a Chartered Financial Analyst (CFA) or a Chartered Financial Consultant (ChFC).

▶ For recommendations, visit the Financial Planning Association Web site, www.fpanet.org, or the National Association of Personal Financial Advisors, www.napfa.org.

Quiz

1 After a major life event, you should:

a	Always change your portfolio.
b	Re-evaluate your investment goals and risk tolerance.
c	Do nothing.

Answers to this quiz can be found on page 280

2 If you want to work with a financial advisor, what's the first thing you should do?

a	Decide what you're looking for—a comprehensive plan or help with a specific issue.
b	Set up a meeting with a handful of candidates.
c	Request references from some advisors.

3 What is an ADV form?

a	The contract you sign with an advisor.
b	The advisor's bill.
c	The advisor's resume.

4 To determine how quickly a company is growing, examine its:

a	Sales growth.
b	Cash flows.
c	Return on assets.

5 To determine how profitable a company is, examine its:

a	Sales growth.
b	Cash flows.
c	Return on assets.

Worksheet

How have you refined your portfolio in the past to account for lifestyle changes such as marriage, children, college tuition, and so on? Have you handled these shifts on your own or with the help of an advisor?

What are you looking for in a financial advisor? How active a role do you want that person to play in your investment planning?

What kind of compensation does your advisor receive? (If you haven't asked him or her before, it's time to do so.) Does your advisor have ties to specific fund families? Is your advisor limited in what he or she can recommend as a result?

Investing Terms

A

Alpha

A measure of the difference between a fund's actual returns and its expected performance, given its level of risk as measured by beta. A positive alpha figure indicates the fund has performed better than its beta would predict. In contrast, a negative alpha indicates the fund's underperformance, given the expectations established by the fund's beta. Alpha depends on two factors: the assumption that market risk, as measured by beta, is the only risk measure necessary, and the strength of the linear relationship between the fund and the index, as it has been measured by R-squared.

Annual Returns

Morningstar calculates annual total returns on a calendar-year and year-to-date basis. The year-to-date return is updated daily on Morningstar.com. For mutual funds, return includes both income (in the form of dividends or interest payments) and capital gains or losses (the increase or decrease in the value of a security). Morningstar calculates total return by taking the change in a fund's NAV, assuming the reinvment of all income and capital-gains distributions (on the actual reinvestment date used by the fund) during the period, and then dividing by the initial NAV. Unless total returns are marked as load adjusted, Morningstar does not adjust total return for sales charges or for redemption fees. Total returns do account for management, administrative, and 12b-1 fees and other costs automatically deducted from fund assets.

Automatic-Investment Plan

An arrangement by which investors may initiate an account with a fund with a very small investment up front, with the condition that they agree to invest a fixed amount per month in the future.

Average Credit Quality/Credit Quality

In Morningstar.com products, average credit quality gives a snapshot of the portfolio's overall credit quality. It is an average of each bond's credit rating, adjusted for its relative weighting in the portfolio. For corporate-bond and municipal-bond funds, Morningstar also shows the percentage of fixed-income securities that fall within each credit-quality rating, as assigned by Standard & Poor's or Moody's. U.S. government bonds carry the highest credit rating, while bonds issued by speculative or bankrupt companies usually carry the lowest credit ratings. Anything at or below BB is considered a high-yield or "junk" bond.

Average Weighted Price

Morningstar generates this figure from the fund's portfolio by weighting the price of each bond by its relative size in the portfolio. This number reveals if the fund favors bonds selling at prices above or below face value (premium or discount securities, respectively). A higher number indicates a bias toward premiums. This statistic is expressed as a percentage of par (face) value. Average weighted price can reflect current market expectations. Morningstar generates this figure from the fund's portfolio, by weighting the price of each bond by its relative size in the portfolio.

B

Bear Market

A period when investment values drop. Bear markets can exist for certain kinds of investments (such as small-company stocks), for an index (such as the S&P 500), or marketwide. Bear markets usually aren't labeled as such until values have slipped by 20%. Its opposite is called a bull market.

Bear Market % Rank

In Morningstar products, the bear-market percentile rank details how a fund has performed during bear markets. For stock funds, a bear market is defined as all months in the past five years that the S&P 500 lost more than 3%; for bond funds, it's all months in the past five years that the Lehman Brothers Aggregate Bond Index lost more than 1%. Morningstar adds a fund's performance during each bear-market month to arrive at a total bear-market return. Based on these returns, each fund is then assigned a percentile ranking. Stock funds are ranked separately from bond funds. Use this figure to analyze how well a fund performs during market downturns, relative to its peers.

Benchmark

What you compare your fund's returns with to judge its performance. A benchmark can be the average performance of funds similar to yours or a broad index of the investments your fund usually picks from. The S&P 500 Index is a good benchmark for funds that buy large-company stocks, for example.

Best Fit Alpha

In Morningstar products, this is the alpha of the fund relative to its Best Fit Index. Alpha is a measure of the difference between a fund's actual returns and its expected performance given its level of risk as measured by beta. A positive alpha figure indicates the fund has performed better than its beta would predict. In contrast, a negative alpha indicates the fund has underperformed given the expectations established by its beta.

Best Fit Beta

On Morningstar.com, this is the beta of the fund relative to its Best Fit Index. Beta is a measure of a fund's sensitivity to market movements. The beta of the market is 1.00 by definition. Morningstar calculates beta by comparing a fund's excess return over Treasury bills to the Best Fit Index's excess return over Treasury bills. A beta of 1.10 shows that the fund has performed 10% better than its Best Fit Index in up markets and 10% worse in down markets, assuming all other factors remained constant.

Best Fit Index

Morningstar defines this as the market index that shows the highest correlation with a fund over the most recent 36 months, as measured by the highest R-squared. Morningstar regresses a fund's monthly excess returns against the monthly excess returns of several well-known market indexes. Both the standard and best-fit results can be useful to investors. The standard index R-squared statistics can help investors plan the diversification of their portfolio of funds. For example, an investor who wishes to diversify and already owns a fund with a very high correlation (and thus high R-squared) with the S&P 500 might choose not to buy another fund that correlates closely to that index. In addition, the best-fit index can be used to compare the betas and alphas of similar funds that show the same best-fit index. Morningstar recalculates the best-fit index in-house on a monthly basis.

Beta

A measure of a fund's sensitivity to market movements. The beta of the market is 1.00 by definition. Morningstar calculates beta by comparing a fund's excess return over Treasury bills to the market's excess return over Treasury bills, so a beta of 1.10 shows that the fund has performed 10% better than its benchmark index in up markets and 10% worse in down markets, assuming all other factors remain constant. Conversely, a beta of 0.85 indicates that the fund is expected to perform 15% worse than the market during up markets and 15% better during down markets. Beta can be a useful tool when at least some of a fund's performance history can be explained by the market as a whole. Beta is particularly appropriate when used to measure the risk of a combined portfolio of mutual funds. It is important to note that a low beta for a fund does not necessarily imply that the fund has a low level of volatility. A low beta signifies only that the fund's market-related risk is low.

Bond

A loan you make to a company or government for a certain time (the bond's term or maturity) typically in return for regular interest payments (the bond's coupon). Interest from some government bonds, particularly municipal bonds, may be tax-free.

Broker

The "intermediary" between you and the other investors, a broker buys and sells securities for you for a fee, called a commission. There are many kinds of brokers, from online brokers, who allow you to trade cheaply over the Internet, to full-service brokers, who provide advice and other services.

Bull Market

A good time for investors! Stock prices rise during a bull market. And when stock prices go up, investors (usually) make money. Investors who think the stock market will continue to go up are called bulls. The opposite of a bull market is called a bear market.

C

Capital Appreciation

A gain in the value of a stock or bond. The amount of appreciation is measured by subtracting the purchase price from the current price.

Capital Gain/Loss

The difference between what you pay for a stock or other investment and what you sell it for. In other words, your profit or loss. If you buy shares of Great Company for $100 and sell them for $250, your capital gain is $150. You pay taxes on capital gains.

Cash Flow

Basically, what a company makes minus what it spends. A company's cash flow is its income (minus investment earnings) less what it spends on rent, equipment, and other costs. Some investors use cash flow instead of earnings to judge how well a company is doing.

Closed-End Funds

An investment that acts like a cross between a mutual fund and a stock. Like a mutual fund, it invests a pool of money in a variety of investments. Like a stock, however, it issues a limited number of shares that can trade at prices different from the value of its investments.

Closed Fund

An open-end fund that has closed, either temporarily or permanently, to new investors. This usually occurs when management finds the fund's increasing asset size to be disadvantageous.

Closed to All Investments

Funds that are accepting no investments whatsoever, even from current shareholders.

Closed to New Investments

If funds are closed to new investments, they are not accepting new shareholder investments. This does not, however, restrict current shareholders from increasing their investment amount.

Commission

What you pay a broker or financial advisor to buy or sell investments for you. Commissions can be a percentage of your trade (for example, 5% of a $10,000 trade equals a $500 commission) or a set fee. You usually pay a higher commission the more services your broker provides.

Composition

The composition percentages on Morningstar.com provide a simple breakdown of a fund's portfolio holdings, as of the date listed, into general investment classes. Cash encompasses both the actual cash and the cash equivalents (fixed-income securities with maturities of one year or less) held by the portfolio. Negative percentages of cash indicate that the portfolio is leveraged, meaning it has borrowed against its own assets to buy more securities or that it has used other techniques to gain additional exposure to the market.

Compounding

When your interest earns interest. If you invest $10,000 and generate a return of 10%, you'll have $11,000 at the end of the year. If you earn 10% again the next year, both your initial investment and your $1,000 in interest earn interest, for a new total of $12,100. Over time, compounding's effect is powerful.

Coupon

The fixed percentage paid out on a fixed-income security on an annual basis.

Credit Analysis

For corporate-bond and municipal-bond funds, the credit analysis depicts the quality of bonds in the fund's portfolio. The analysis reveals the percentage of fixed-income securities that fall within each credit-quality rating as assigned by Standard & Poor's or Moody's. At the top of the ratings are U.S. government bonds. Bonds issued and backed by the federal government are of extremely high quality and thus are considered superior to bonds rated AAA, which is the highest possible rating a corporate issue can receive. Morningstar gives U.S. government bonds a credit rating separate from AAA securities to allow for a more accurate credit analysis of a portfolio's holdings. Bonds with a BBB rating are the lowest bonds that are still considered to be of investment grade. Bonds that are rated BB or lower (often called junk bonds or high-yield bonds) are considered to be quite speculative. Like the style box, the credit analysis can help determine whether or not a fund's portfolio meets a desired standard or quality. It can also shed light on the management strategy of the fund. If the fund holds a large percentage of assets in lower-quality issues, for example, then the fund follows a more aggressive style and is probably more concerned with yield than credit quality.

Credit Risk

The chance that you won't be able to get interest payments or your money back from the issuer that sold you a bond. Government bonds have low credit risk, while junk bonds from companies with shaky credit have high credit risk.

D

Developed Markets

Morningstar characterizes the following as developed markets: Australia, Austria, Belgium, Canada, Denmark, Finland, France, Germany, Ireland, Italy, Japan, Luxembourg, the Netherlands, New Zealand, Norway, Singapore, Spain, Sweden, Switzerland, the United Kingdom, the United States, and a handful of smaller countries and territories (such as Gibraltar). All other countries are considered emerging markets. Emerging markets normally carry greater political and economic risk than developed countries, and stocks located in them are normally less liquid and more volatile.

Diversification

Spreading your money over many different investments. When you're diversified, if one investment does badly for a while, you may still make money from your other investments. Diversification generally lowers risk.

Dividends

Money taken from a company's profits and paid to stockholders. Companies aren't required to pay dividends. Dividends are paid to you either in cash or in more stock. Mutual funds that own dividend-paying stock must pass the dividends along to their shareholders each year.

Dollar-Cost Averaging

A way to buy more of an investment when it's cheaper and less when it's expensive. To dollar-cost average, you simply invest the same amount of money every week, month, or paycheck so that, as an investment's price falls, you automatically buy more shares.

Duration

One measure of the interest-rate sensitivity of a bond or bond fund. Bond funds with long durations will do well when interest rates are declining but suffer as interest rates rise. Short-duration bond funds are less volatile but offer fewer potential gains.

E

Earnings-per-Share Growth %

This figure for Morningstar products represents the annualized rate of net-income-per-share growth over the trailing one-year period for the stocks held by a fund. Earnings-per-share growth gives a good picture of the rate at which a company has grown its profitability per unit of equity. All things being equal, stocks with higher earnings-per-share growth rates are generally more desirable than those with slower earnings-per-share growth rates. One of the important differences between earnings-per-share growth rates and net-income growth rates is that the former reflects the dilution that occurs from new stock issuance, the exercise of employee stock options, warrants, convertible securities, and share repurchases.

Emerging Markets

Morningstar characterizes the following as developed markets: Australia, Austria, Belgium, Canada, Denmark, Finland, France, Germany, Ireland, Italy, Japan, Luxembourg, the Netherlands, New Zealand, Norway, Singapore, Spain, Sweden, Switzerland, the United Kingdom, the United States, and a handful of smaller countries and territories (such as Gibraltar). All other countries are considered emerging markets. Emerging markets normally carry greater political and economic risk than developed countries, and stocks located in them are normally less liquid and more volatile.

Enhanced-Index Funds

Like index funds, this group includes funds that attempt to match an index's performance. Unlike an index fund, however, enhanced-index funds typically attempt to better the index by adding value or reducing volatility through selective stock-picking.

Exchange-Traded Funds

At the most basic level, exchange-traded funds are just what their name implies: baskets of securities that are traded, like individual stocks, on an exchange. Unlike regular open-end mutual funds, ETFs are priced throughout the trading day. They can also be sold short and bought on margin—anything you might do with a stock, you can do with an ETF. They often also charge lower annual expenses than even the least costly index mutual funds. However, as with stocks, you must pay a commission to buy and sell ETF shares, which can be a significant drawback for those who trade frequently or invest regular sums of money.

Expense Ratio

The annual expense ratio, taken from the fund's annual report, expresses the percentage of assets deducted each fiscal year for fund expenses, including 12b-1 fees, management fees, administrative fees, operating costs, and all other asset-based costs incurred by the fund. Portfolio transaction fees, or brokerage costs, as well as initial or deferred sales charges are not included in the expense ratio. The expense ratio, which is deducted from the fund's average net assets, is accrued on a daily basis. Funds may also opt to waive all or a portion of the expenses that make up their overall expense ratio. The expense ratio is useful because it shows the actual amount that a fund takes out of its assets each year to cover its expenses. Investors should note not only the current expense-ratio figure, but also the trend in these expenses; it could prove useful to know whether a fund is becoming cheaper or more costly. Overall, expenses can have a meaningful impact on long-term results, so investors should try to invest in funds with below-average expenses.

F

Fees and Expenses

Morningstar distinguishes among the myriad fees and expenses encountered with mutual funds. The different expenses and their characteristics are listed as follows.

12b-1—The 12b-1 fee represents the maximum annual charge deducted from fund assets to pay for distribution and marketing costs. This fee is expressed as a percentage. Some funds may be permitted to impose 12b-1 fees but are currently waiving all or a portion of the fees. Total allowable 12b-1 fees, excluding loads, are capped at 1% of average net assets annually. Of this, the distribution and marketing portion of the fee may account for up to 0.75%. The other portion of the overall 12b-1 fee, the service fee, is listed separately and may account for up to 0.25%. Often, funds charging a 12b-1 fee will allow shareholders to convert into a share class without the fee after a certain number of years. (These are normally deferred-load funds.)

Administrative Costs—What your fund charges you in order to pay for its day-to-day operations, including renting office space, printing prospectuses, and keeping records. You'll never write a check for this fee, though, because administrative costs, like the other parts of your fund's expense ratio, are deducted directly from your fund's returns.

Deferred Load—Also called a contingent deferred sales charge or back-end load, a deferred load is an alternative to the traditional front-end sales charge, as it is deducted only at the time of sale of fund shares. The deferred-load structure commonly decreases to zero over a period of time. A typical deferred load's structure might have a 5% charge if shares are redeemed within the first year of ownership and decline by a percentage point each year thereafter. These loads are normally applied to the lesser of original share price or current market value. It is important to note that although the deferred load declines each year, the accumulated annual distribution and services charges (the total 12b-1 fee) usually offset this decline.

Front-End Load—The initial sales charge or front-end load is a deduction made from each investment in the fund. The amount is generally based on the amount of the investment. Larger investments, both initial and cumulative, generally receive percentage discounts based on the dollar value invested. A typical front-end load might have a 4.75% charge for purchases less than $50,000, which decreases as the amount of the investment increases. Investors who have significant assets and work with a financial advisor are therefore better off buying front-load shares than deferred-load shares.

Management Fee—The management fee is the maximum percentage deducted from a fund's average net assets to pay an advisor or subadvisor. Often, as the fund's net assets grow, the percentage deducted for management fees decreases. Alternatively, the fund may compute the fee as a flat percentage of average net assets. A portion of the management fee may also be charged in the form of a group fee. To determine the group fee, the fund family creates a sliding scale for the family's total net assets and determines a percentage applied to each fund's asset base. The management fee might also be amended by or be primarily composed of a perform-

ance fee, which raises or lowers the management fee based on the fund's returns relative to an established index.

No-Load—These funds charge no sales or 12b-1 fees.

Redemption Fee—The redemption fee is an amount charged when money is withdrawn from the fund before a predetermined period elapses. This fee usually does not go back into the pockets of the fund company, but rather into the fund itself and thus does not represent a net cost to shareholders. Also, unlike contingent-deferred sales charges, redemption fees typically operate only in short, specific time clauses, commonly 30, 180, or 365 days. However, some redemption fees exist for up to five years. Charges are not imposed after the stated time has passed. These fees are typically imposed to discourage market-timers, whose quick movements into and out of funds can be disruptive. The charge is normally imposed on the ending share value, appreciated or depreciated from the original value.

Service Fee—The service fee is part of the total 12b-1 fee. Capped at a maximum 0.25%, the service fee is designed to compensate financial planners or brokers for ongoing shareholder-liaison services, which may include responding to customer inquiries and providing information on investments. An integral component of level-load and deferred-load funds, the fees were previously known as a trail commission. Only service fees adopted pursuant to Rule 12b-1 are tracked. Despite the implication of its name, service fees do not act as compensation for transfer agency or custodial services.

Fixed Income

An investment that pays a specific interest rate, such as a bond, a certificate of deposit, or preferred stock. Mutual funds composed of fixed-income instruments (like bond funds) typically pay a variable rate of interest.

401(k) Plan

An employer-sponsored retirement plan. It lets you invest part of your paycheck—before taxes are deducted—in investments, such as mutual funds, that you choose from the plan. Your 401(k) money isn't taxed until you start withdrawing it, usually at retirement.

Fund Advisor

This is the company or companies that are given primary responsibility for managing a fund's portfolio.

Fund Family

A fund family is a company that offers mutual funds. Generally speaking, the company name is included in the official fund name.

Fund Inception Date

The date on which the fund began its operations. Funds with long track records offer more history by which investors can assess overall fund performance. However, another important factor to consider is the fund manager and his or her tenure with the fund. Often a change in fund performance can indicate a change in management.

Fund of Funds

A mutual fund that invests in other mutual funds. The goal is to give you maximum diversification with a single investment. You might think of it as buying an assortment of chocolates in a box, rather than separately. One difference: With a fund of funds, you often pay extra for the "box."

G

Growth Measures

Long-Term Earnings Growth—Earnings are what is left of a firm's revenues after it pays all of its expenses, costs, and taxes. Companies whose earnings grow faster than those of their industry peers usually see better price performance for their stocks. Projected earnings growth is an estimate of a company's expected long-term growth in earnings, derived from all polled analysts' estimates. When reported for a mutual fund, it shows the weighted average of the projected growth in earnings for each stock in the fund's portfolio. This measure helps determine Morningstar's growth score for each stock and the overall growth orientation of the fund.

Historical Earnings Growth—Historical earnings growth shows the rate of increase in a company's earnings per share, based on up to four periodic time periods. When reported for a mutual fund, it shows the weighted average of the growth in earnings for each stock in the fund's portfolio. This measure helps determine Morningstar's growth score for each stock and the overall growth orientation of the fund.

Sales Growth—Sales growth shows the rate of increase in a company's sales per share, based on up to four periodic time periods and is considered the best gauge of how rapidly a company's core business is growing. When reported for a mutual fund, it shows the weighted average of the sales-growth rates for each stock in the fund's portfolio. This measure helps determine Morningstar's growth score for each stock and the overall growth orientation of the fund.

Cash-Flow Growth—Cash flow tells you how much cash a business is actually generating from its earnings before depreciation, amortization, and noncash charges. Sometimes called cash earnings, it's considered a gauge of liquidity and solvency. Cash-flow growth shows the rate of increase in a company's cash flow per share, based on up to four time periods. When reported for a mutual fund, it shows the weighted average of the growth in cash flow for each stock in the fund's portfolio. This measure helps determine Morningstar's growth score for each stock and the overall growth orientation of the fund.

Book-Value Growth—Book value is, in theory, what would be left over for shareholders if a company shut down its operations, paid off all its creditors, collected from all its debtors, and liquidated itself. In practice, however, the value of assets and liabilities can change substantially from when they are first recorded. Book-value growth shows the rate of increase in a company's book value per share, based on up to four periodic time periods. When reported for a mutual fund, it shows the weighted average of the growth rates in book value for each stock in the fund's portfolio. This measure helps determine Morningstar's growth score for each stock and the overall growth orientation of the fund.

Growth of $10,000 Graph—The Growth of $10,000 graph shows a fund's performance based on how $10,000 invested in a fund would have grown over time. The returns used in the graph are not load-adjusted. The growth of $10,000 begins at the date of the fund's inception, or the first year listed on the graph, whichever is appropriate.

H

Hedge Fund

A hedge fund is like a mutual fund on steroids. Most hedge funds have really high minimum investments, often $1 million or more, and are allowed to make risky investments that mutual funds aren't. Hence, they can make and lose lots of money.

I

Index Funds

Funds that track a particular index and attempt to match its returns. While an index typically has a much larger portfolio than a mutual fund, the fund's management may study the index's movements to develop a representative sampling and match sectors proportionately.

Individual Retirement Account (IRA)

A tax-deferred retirement account that permits individuals to set aside tax-deferred earnings each year. IRAs can be established at a bank, mutual fund, or brokerage.

Institutional Funds

A mutual fund that generally only sells shares to big players such as pension plans. The typical institutional fund has a high minimum investment, typically $100,000 or more. You may be able to get into an institutional fund for less through online brokers or an employer retirement plan.

Interest-Rate Sensitivity

How much the value of a bond or bond fund changes when interest rates shift. Bond values move in the opposite direction from interest rates. Duration is one common measure of interest-rate sensitivity.

L

Life-cycle Funds

These funds are designed to be an investor's sole investment. Usually designated as aggressive, moderate, or conservative, these funds typically hold a mix of stocks and bonds.

Liquidity

A way to describe how easily you can sell an investment for cash. Your savings account, for instance, has lots of liquidity because you can get at your money anytime. Stocks that are traded a lot are also very liquid. Little-known stocks and most collectibles are considered illiquid.

M

Management Team

This applies to funds in which there are two or more people involved in fund management, and they manage together, or when the fund strongly promotes its team-managed aspect.

Manager Tenure

This represents the number of years that the current manager has been the portfolio manager of the fund. Fund management is clearly an important variable in fund performance. If you buy a fund for its long-term performance,

for example, you'll want to be sure that the manager responsible for the good record is still at his or her post. Likewise, if an improvement in fund performance correlates with the arrival of a new manager, investors should downplay the fund's previous record and focus on the performance attributable to the new management.

Market Capitalization

For domestic-stock offerings, this measures the portfolio's "center of gravity," in terms of the size of companies in which it invests. A market capitalization is calculated for each stock. Its weight in the average weighted market-cap calculation is then determined by the percentage of stocks it consumes in the overall portfolio. For example, a stock that is a 10% position in a fund will have twice as much influence on the calculation than a stock that is a 5% stake.

Market-Neutral Funds

These are funds that attempt to eliminate the risks of the market, typically by holding 50% of assets in long positions in stocks and 50% of assets in short positions. Funds in this group match the characteristics of their long and short portfolios, keeping factors such as P/E ratios and industry exposure similar. Stock-picking, rather than broad market moves, should drive a market-neutral fund's performance.

Market Risk

The chance that an entire group of investments, such as U.S. stocks, will lose value (as opposed to one particular stock falling in price). Market risk is a danger because there's always the chance you'll have to sell an investment when the market is down.

Market-Timing

This is an investment strategy in which investors switch in and out of securities or between types of mutual funds in the hopes of benefiting from various economic and technical indicators that are thought to presage market moves.

Market Value

The current value of the security. For stocks, the market value is the security price times the number of shares held. For bonds, the market value is the bond price multiplied by the number of bonds held.

Maturity

How long you must wait before a bond repays you. For instance, a 30-year bond pays you interest for 30 years, then repays you your investment, or principal. The longer the maturity, the riskier the bond, because you must wait longer before reinvesting your money.

Mean

Represents the annualized total return for a fund over 3-, 5-, and 10-year time periods.

Minimum Investments

Initial Investment—The minimum purchase indicates the smallest investment amount a fund will accept to establish a new account.

Additional Investment—This indicates the smallest additional purchase amount a fund will accept in an existing account.

Initial Auto-Invest Program Investment—This indicates the smallest amount with which one may enter a fund's automatic-investment plan—an arrangement in which the fund takes money on a monthly, quarterly, semi-annual, or annual basis from the shareholder's checking account. The systematic investment amount is the minimum amount required for subsequent regular investments in an automatic investment plan. Studies indicate that regular automatic investment, also known as dollar-cost averaging, is perhaps the most successful investment plan for long-term investors.

Additional Auto-Invest Program Investment—This indicates the smallest additional investment amount a fund will accept in an existing automatic-investment plan account.

Money Market—Similar to a savings account, only usually paying you a better interest rate. Money-market funds invest in extremely short-term instruments. As a result, they're ultrasafe and you can withdraw exactly what you've deposited at any time.

Morningstar Category

While the investment objective stated in a fund's prospectus may or may not reflect how the fund actually invests, a Morningstar category is assigned based on the underlying securities in each portfolio. Morningstar categories help investors and investment professionals make meaningful comparisons between funds. The categories make it easier to build well-diversified portfolios, assess potential risk, and identify top-performing funds. We place funds in a given category based on their portfolio statistics and compositions over the past three years. If the fund is new and has no portfolio history, we estimate where it will fall before giving it a more permanent category assignment. When necessary, we may change a category assignment based on recent changes to the portfolio.

Domestic-Stock Funds—Funds with at least 70% of assets in domestic stocks are categorized based on the style and size of the stocks they typically own. The style and size divisions reflect those used in the Morningstar style box: value, blend, or growth style and small, medium, or large median market capitalization.

International-Stock Funds—Stock funds that have invested 40% or more of their equity holdings in foreign stocks (on average over the past three years) are placed in one of the following international-stock categories:

Europe—At least 75% of stocks invested in Europe.

Japan—At least 75% of stocks invested in Japan.

Latin America—At least 75% of stocks invested in Latin America.

Diversified Pacific—At least 65% of stocks invested in Pacific countries, with at least an additional 10% of stocks invested in Japan.

Asia/Pacific ex-Japan—At least 75% of stocks invested in Pacific countries, with less than 10% of stocks invested in Japan.

Diversified Emerging Markets—At least 50% of stocks invested in emerging markets.

Foreign—An international fund having no more than 20% of stocks invested in the United States.

World—An international fund having more than 20% of stocks invested in the United States.

World Allocation—Used for funds with stock holdings of greater than 20% but less than 70% of the portfolio where 40% of the stocks and bonds are foreign.

Bond Funds—Funds with 80% or more of their assets invested in bonds are classified as bond funds. Bond funds are divided into two main groups: taxable bond and municipal bond. (Note: For all bond funds, maturity figures are used only when duration figures are unavailable.)

Taxable-Bond Funds
Long-Term Government—A fund with at least 90% of bond portfolio invested in government issues with a duration of greater than or equal to 6 years, or an average effective maturity of greater than 10 years.

Intermediate-Term Government—A fund with at least 90% of its bond portfolio invested in government issues with a duration of greater than or equal to 3.5 years and less than 6 years, or an average effective maturity of greater than or equal to 4 years and less than 10 years.

Short-Term Government—A fund with at least 90% of its bond portfolio invested in government issues with a duration of greater than or equal to one year and less than 3.5 years, or average effective maturity of greater than or equal to one year and less than four years.

Long-Term Bond—A fund that focuses on corporate and other investment-grade issues with an average duration of more than 6 years, or an average effective maturity of more than 10 years.

Intermediate-Term Bond—A fund that focuses on corporate, government, foreign, or other issues with an average duration of greater than or equal to 3.5 years but less than or equal to 6 years, or an average effective maturity of more than 4 years but less than 10 years.

Short-Term Bond—A fund that focuses on corporate and other investment-grade issues with an average duration of more than one year but less than 3.5 years, or an average effective maturity of more than one year but less than four years.

Ultrashort Bond—Used for funds with an average duration or an average effective maturity of less than one year. This category includes general- and government-bond funds, and excludes any international, convertible, multisector, and high-yield bond funds.

Bank Loan—A fund that invests primarily in floating-rate bank loans instead of bonds. In exchange for their credit risk, these funds offer high interest payments that typically float above a common short-term benchmark.

World Bond—A fund that invests at least 40% of bonds in foreign markets.

Emerging-Markets Bond—A fund that invests at least 65% of assets in emerging-markets bonds.

High-Yield Bond—A fund with at least 65% of assets in bonds rated below BBB.

Multisector Bond—Used for funds that seek income by diversifying their assets among several fixed-income sectors, usually U.S. government obligations, foreign bonds, and high-yield domestic debt securities.

Municipal-Bond Funds
Municipal National Long-Term—A national fund with an average duration of more than 7 years, or average maturity of more than 12 years.

Municipal National Intermediate-Term— A national fund with an average duration of more than 4.5 years but less than 7 years, or average maturity of more than 5 years but less than 12 years.

High-Yield Municipal—A fund that invests at least 50% of assets in high-income municipal securities that are not rated or that are rated by a major rating agency at the level of BBB (considered speculative in the municipal industry) or below.

Municipal National Short—A fund that focuses on municipal bonds with an average duration of less than 4.5 years, or an average maturity of less than 5 years.

State-Specific Munis—A municipal-bond fund that primarily invests in one specific state. These funds must have at least 80% of assets invested in municipal bonds from that state. Each state-specific muni category includes long, intermediate, and short-duration bond funds.

Morningstar Rating for Funds
A measure of how well a mutual fund has balanced risk and return. We compare a fund's long-term risk-adjusted performance with that of its category peers. A 5-star rating is the best; 1 star is the worst.

Morningstar Risk

An assessment of the variations in a fund's monthly returns, with an emphasis on downside variations, in comparison to similar funds. In each Morningstar Category, the 10% of funds with the lowest measured risk are described as Low Risk, the next 22.5% Below Average, the middle 35% Average, the next 22.5% Above Average, and the top 10% High. Morningstar Risk is measured for up to three time periods (3, 5, and 10 years). These separate measures are then weighted and averaged to produce an overall measure for the fund. Funds with less than three years of performance history are not rated.

Multiple Managers

This refers to the arrangement in which two or more people are involved in the fund management, and they manage independently; quite often the fund has divided net assets in set amounts among the individual managers. In most cases, multiple managers are employed at different subadvisors or investment firms.

Mutual Fund

An investment company that sells shares to people and uses the money to buy stocks, bonds, and other investments. The mutual fund passes on the earnings from its investments to its shareholders. Mutual funds are an easy way for individuals to invest in a lot of securities at once.

N

NAV

A fund's net asset value (NAV) represents its per-share price. A fund's NAV is derived by dividing the total net assets of the fund, less fees and expenses, by the number of shares outstanding.

Net Income Growth %

This figure for Morningstar products represents the annualized rate of net-income growth over the trailing one-year period for the stocks held by a fund. Net-income growth gives a good picture of the rate at which companies have grown their profits. All things being equal, stocks with higher net-income growth rates are generally more desirable than those with slower net-income growth rates. Morningstar aggregates net-income growth figures for mutual funds using a median methodology, whereby domestic stocks are ordered from highest to lowest based on their net-income growth rates. One adds up the asset weighting of each holding until the total is equal to or greater than half of the total weighting of all domestic stocks in the fund. The net-income growth rate for that stock is then used to represent the net-income growth rate of the total portfolio.

P

Portfolio

All the investments you own or, similarly, all the investments your fund owns.

Potential Capital-Gains Exposure

The percentage of a fund's total assets that represent capital appreciation. In other words, this is how much of the fund's assets would be subject to taxation if the fund were to liquidate today. Where a negative number appears, the fund has reported losses on its books. This information (realized and unrealized appreciation and net assets) is taken from the fund's annual report. Although funds rarely liquidate their entire portfolio, a fund with a higher potential capital gains exposure may be more likely to realize large capital gains in the event of a manager change or strategy shift. A high capital-gains exposure often accompanies a low turnover strategy, wherein a fund holds stocks over the long term, allowing profits to accumulate.

Price/Book Ratio

The price/book (P/B) ratio of a fund is the weighted average of the price/book ratios of all the stocks in a fund's portfolio. Book value is the total assets of a company, less total liabilities (sometimes referred to as carrying value). A company's price/book value is calculated by dividing the market price of its outstanding stock by the company's book value, and then adjusting for the number of shares outstanding. (Stocks with negative book values are excluded from this calculation.)

Price/Cash-Flow Ratio

This represents the weighted average of the price/cash-flow ratios of the stocks in a fund's portfolio. Price/cash-flow represents the amount an investor is willing to pay for a dollar generated from a particular company's operations. Price/cash-flow shows the ability of a business to generate cash and acts as a gauge of liquidity and solvency. Because accounting conventions differ among nations, reported earnings (and P/E ratios) may not be comparable across national boundaries. Price/cash-flow attempts to provide an internationally standard measure of a firm's stock price relative to its financial performance.

Price/Earnings Ratio

The price/earnings (P/E) ratio of a fund is the weighted average of the price/earnings ratios of the stocks in a fund's portfolio. The P/E ratio of a company, which is a comparison of the cost of the company's stock and its trailing 12-month earnings per share, is calculated by dividing a stock's price by its earnings. In computing the average, Morningstar weights each portfolio holding by the percentage of equity assets it represents, so that larger positions have proportionately greater influence on the fund's final P/E. A high P/E usually indicates that the market will pay more to obtain the company's earnings because it believes in the firm's ability to increase its earnings. (P/ES can also be artificially inflated if a company has very weak trailing earnings, and thus a very small number in this equation's denominator.) A low P/E indicates the market has less confidence that the company's earnings will increase; however, a fund manager or an individual with a 'value investing' approach may believe such stocks have an overlooked or undervalued potential for appreciation.

Price/Sales Ratio

This represents the weighted average of the price/sales ratios of the stocks in a fund's portfolio. Price/sales represents the amount an investor is willing to pay for a dollar generated from a particular company's operations.

Prime-Rate Funds

These funds invest in senior corporate loans and senior secured debt securities. These funds anticipate paying dividends that float or reset at a margin above a generally recognized rate such as LIBOR (London Inter-Bank Offer Rate).

Principal

The money you originally invested. It can also mean the face value of a bond, which you get back when the bond matures. You don't count income or capital gains as principal for an investment, even if you reinvest them.

Projected Earnings Growth %

This figure on Morningstar.com represents the projected one-year earnings growth rate of the stocks held by a fund. Projected earnings growth gives a good picture of a company's growth projects. All things being equal, stocks with better growth prospects are more desirable than those with poorer growth rates. Morningstar aggregates projected earnings growth figures for mutual funds using a median methodology, whereby domestic stocks are ordered from highest to lowest based on their projected earnings growth. One adds up the asset weighting of each holding until the total is equal to or greater than half of the total weighting of all domestic stocks in the fund. The projected earnings growth rate for that stock is then used to represent the projected one-year earnings growth rate of the total portfolio.

Prospectus

A guide legally required by the SEC that explains many of the details about a mutual fund. Always read the prospectus before making an investment. A mutual fund's prospectus will tell you how the fund picks investments, how much it has made in the past, and what its major risks are.

Q

Qualified Access

This is any fund offered through a retirement plan such as an employee pension plan, 401(k), or 403(b) plan. These plans meet the necessary IRS requirements to allow participants to deduct the amount of their investments from their taxable income, thereby investing pretax dollars. Money builds up on a tax-deferred basis, and when the investor withdraws money, both the principal and profit are treated as taxable income.

R

Return

The amount of money your investment made for you. Usually return is given as a percentage of the amount you invested, so a $5,000 investment that made you $400 earned an 8% return ($400 divided by $5,000).

Revenue Growth

This figure represents the rate of revenue growth over the trailing one-year period for the stocks held by a fund. Revenue growth gives a good picture of the rate at which companies have been able to expand their businesses. All things being equal, stocks with higher revenue growth rates are generally more desirable than those with slower revenue growth rates.

Role in Portfolio

Morningstar designates funds as core, supporting player, or specialty. Core funds should be the bulk of an investor's portfolio, while supporting players contribute to a portfolio but are secondary to the core. Specialty offerings tend to be speculative and should typically only be a small portion of investors' portfolios.

R-Squared

The percentage of an investment's returns explained by movements in a benchmark index. An S&P 500 index fund will have an R-squared of nearly 100 compared with the S&P 500 Index, since they move in step, but would have a much lower one compared with a gold index.

S

Sector Fund

A mutual fund that invests in companies in a specific type of business. Sector funds can invest in a general industry, such as technology companies, or a specific industry, such as Internet companies. Because they focus on only one industry, they're usually riskier than general stock funds.

Sector Risk

The danger that the stock of many of the companies in one sector (such as health care or technology) will fall in price at the same time because of an event that affects the entire industry.

Shareholder Report

A guide your mutual fund sends out at least twice per year with information on how the fund is doing and what investments it owns. It usually includes a letter from your fund's president and/or manager.

Sharpe Ratio

This risk-adjusted measure was developed by Nobel Laureate William Sharpe. It is calculated by using standard deviation and excess return to determine reward per unit of risk. The higher the Sharpe ratio, the better the fund's historical risk-adjusted performance. The Sharpe ratio is calculated for the past 36-month period by dividing a fund's annualized excess returns over the risk-free rate by its annualized standard deviation. It is recalculated on a monthly basis. Since this ratio uses standard deviation as its risk measure, it is most appropriately applied when analyzing a fund that is an investor's sole holding. The Sharpe ratio can be used to compare directly how much risk two funds each had to bear to earn excess return over the risk-free rate.

Socially Responsible Funds

These funds, also known as SRI funds, invest according to noneconomic guidelines. Funds may make investments based on such issues as environmental responsibility, human rights, or religious views. For example, socially responsible funds may take a proactive stance by selectively investing in environmentally friendly companies or firms with good employee relations. This group also includes funds that avoid investing in companies involved in promoting alcohol, tobacco, or gambling, or those in the defense industry.

Standard Deviation

This statistical measurement of dispersion about an average depicts how widely a mutual fund's returns varied over a certain period of time. Investors use the standard deviation of historical performance to try to predict the range of returns that are most likely for a given fund. When a fund has a high standard deviation, the predicted range of performance is wide, implying greater volatility. Standard deviation is most appropriate for measuring the risk of a fund that is an investor's only holding. The figure cannot be combined for more than one fund because the standard deviation for a portfolio of multiple funds is a function of not only the individual standard deviations, but also of the degree of correlation among the funds' returns.

Subadvisor

In some cases, a mutual fund's advisor employs another company, called the subadvisor, to handle the fund's day-to-day management. In these instances, the portfolio manager generally works for the fund's subadvisor, and not the advisor.

T

Target-Retirement Funds

These funds are managed for investors planning to retire—or to begin withdrawing substantial portions of their investments—in a particular year. The funds follow an asset-allocation strategy that grows more conservative as the target date nears.

Taxable Account

An investment account that isn't sheltered from taxes. This means you have to pay taxes on any interest payments or distributions, as well as on any gains you realize when you sell the invest-

ment. With tax-deferred accounts, such as IRAS and 401(k)s, you can postpone the payment of these taxes.

Tax-Adjusted Return

These returns are adjusted for taxes and sales charges and follow the SEC guidelines for calculating returns before sale of shares. The tax-adjusted return shows a fund's annualized after-tax total return for the 5- and 10-year periods, excluding any capital-gains effects that would result from selling the fund at the end of the period. To determine this figure, all income and short-term capital-gains distributions are taxed at the maximum federal rate at the time of distribution. Long-term capital gains are taxed at a 20% rate. The after-tax portion is then reinvested in the fund. State and local taxes are ignored, and only the capital-gains are adjusted for tax-exempt funds, as the income from these funds is nontaxable.

Tax-Cost Ratio

This represents the percentage-point reduction in an annualized return that results from income taxes. The calculation assumes investors pay the maximum federal rate on capital gains and ordinary income. For example, if a fund made short-term capital-gains and income distributions that averaged 10% of its NAV over the past three years, an investor in the 35% tax bracket would have a tax-cost ratio of 3.5 percentage points. The 35% tax rate was used for illustrative purposes. However, our tax-cost calculation uses the maximum income-tax rate that applied during the year in which the distribution was made.

Tax-Deferred

An account that lets you wait before paying taxes on your earnings. Your defined contribution account is tax deferred since you only pay taxes on earnings when you withdraw them, not when you earn them. Because more of your money works for you through compounding, tax deferral allows you to earn more.

Tax-Exempt

Off-limits to the Internal Revenue Service. Few investments are completely tax-exempt. Interest from city bonds, for example, is usually free from federal taxes but may be subject to state taxes. Earnings on Roth IRA investments are tax-exempt because you never pay taxes on them.

Tax-Managed Funds

These funds are managed with a sensitivity to tax ramifications. They try to minimize taxable distributions through various methods.

Total Cost Projections

Found in a fund's prospectus, these figures show how much an investor would expect to pay in expenses—sales charges (loads) and fees—over the next 3, 5, and 10 years, assuming a $10,000 investment that grows by 5% per year with redemption at the end of each time period. Total cost projections are commonly based on the past year's incurred fees or an estimate of the current fiscal year's fees, should a portion of the overall fee structure change as of the printing of the fund's most current prospectus. Newer funds are required to print total cost projections for one- and three-year time periods only since longer-term projections may not be possible to estimate.

Total Return

A fund's gain, in percentage terms, over a specified period of time. Total return consists of any income the fund paid out, plus (or minus) any increase (or decrease) in the value of the portfolio's holdings. We assume reinvestment of income and capital-gains distributions in our calculations. Returns are not adjusted for sales charges or redemption fees.

Trailing 12-Month Yield

Yield is the percentage income your portfolio returned over the past 12 months. It is calculated by taking the weighted average of the yields of the stocks and funds that compose the portfolio. Dividend yield for the underlying stocks and funds is calculated by dividing the total dollar amount the security paid out as income to shareholders by the share price. Note that for mutual funds, the dollar-income value includes interest income from fixed-income securities, dividends from stocks, and realized gains from currency transactions.

Turnover Ratio

This is a measure of the fund's trading activity, which is computed by taking the lesser of purchases or sales (excluding all securities with maturities of less than one year) and dividing by average monthly net assets. A turnover ratio of 100% or more does not necessarily suggest that all securities in the portfolio have been traded. In practical terms, the resulting percentage loosely represents the percentage of the portfolio's holdings that have changed over the past year. A low turnover figure (20% to 30%) would indicate a buy-and-hold strategy. High turnover (more than 100%) would indicate an investment strategy involving considerable buying and selling of securities. Morningstar does not calculate turnover ratios. The figure is culled directly from the financial highlights of the fund's annual report.

V

Volatility

Refers to fluctuations in the performance of an investment. A money-market account with a fixed $1 share price has no volatility, but a mutual fund that invests in stocks might be very volatile. In general, investments that generate large returns are more volatile than investments with lower returns.

Y

Yield

The interest or dividends your investments produce. It doesn't include capital gains, which you may receive when you sell an investment. Yield is figured as a percentage of the investment's worth. A $100 bond yielding 5% pays you $5 a year.

Recommended Readings

Common Sense on Mutual Funds: New Imperatives for the Intelligent Investor by John C. Bogle, 2000. Published by John Wiley & Sons. The best book on funds, period.

Classics: An Investor's Anthology by Charles D. Ellis with James R. Vertin, 1990. Published by Business One Irwin.

Asset Allocation: Balancing Financial Risk by Roger C. Gibson, 2000. Published by McGraw-Hill Trade. An essential text that has influenced a whole generation of financial advisors.

The Intelligent Investor: The Definitive Book on Value Investing, Revised Edition by Benjamin Graham, Jason Zweig, 2003. Published by Harper Business. The wisdom in this book still resonates decades after its publication.

Security Analysis: The Classic 1934 Edition by Benjamin Graham and David L. Dodd, 1996. Published by McGraw-Hill Trade. This book is considered by many top managers to be the bible of investing.

Buffett: The Making of an American Capitalist by Roger Lowenstein, 1996. Published by Main Street Books. A great biography. You cannot call yourself a serious investor and not be a student of Buffett.

One Up on Wall Street: How to Use What You Already Know to Make Money in the Market by Peter Lynch, 2000. Published by Simon & Schuster. This classic is one of the most accessible books on picking individual stocks.

A Random Walk Down Wall Street by Burton G. Malkiel, 2004. Published by WW Norton & Company. Makes the case for indexing and shows how much of what we attribute as brilliance among managers may really be random chance.

The Wall Street Journal Guide to Understanding Money and Investing by Kenneth M. Morris, Virginia B. Morris, and Alan M. Siegel, 2004. Published by Fireside. This user-friendly guide provides novices with solid money and market information.

continued...

The New Commonsense Guide to Mutual Funds by Mary Rowland, 1998. Published by Bloomberg Press. Rowland's guide is the perfect choice if you would rather not spend a lot of time reading about funds—or want to read about them in short, digestible chunks.

The Money Game by Adam Smith, 1976. Published by Vintage. While the attitudes are dated, this remains a great history.

The Only Investment Guide You'll Ever Need by Andrew Tobias, 2002. Published by Harvest Books. A great introduction to thinking about the key trade-offs of personal finance.

The Money Masters and the New Money Masters by John Train, 1994. Published by HarperBusiness. Wonderful introductions to some of the best money managers ever.

Additional Morningstar Resources

In addition to this workbook, Morningstar publishes a number of products about mutual funds. There's something for everyone, from newsletters to sourcebooks. Most can be found at your local library, or by calling Morningstar to start your own subscriptions (866-608-9570).

Morningstar® Mutual Funds™

This twice-monthly report service features full-page financial reports and analysis of 1,600 funds specially selected for building and maintaining balanced portfolios. Our report service is favored by professionals and serious investors and carried in more than 4,000 libraries nationwide. Trial subscriptions are available.

Morningstar® FundInvestor™

Monthly newsletter offers 48 pages of fund investing help—including Morningstar model portfolios, analysis of funds, funds to avoid, the FundInvestor 500, and Morningstar Analyst Picks.

Morningstar.com

Our Web site features investing information on funds, stocks, bonds, retirement planning, and more. In addition to powerful portfolio tools, you'll find daily articles by Morningstar analysts and editors. Much information on the site is free, and there's a reasonably priced Premium Membership service for investors requiring more in-depth information and sophisticated analytical tools.

Morningstar® Funds 500™

Annual book of full-page reports on 500 selected funds. The new edition appears in January of each year and includes complete year-end results of funds covered, as well as general fund industry performance information.

Morningstar Guide to Mutual Funds
5-Star Strategies for Success

Here's the perfect desktop resource for new and experienced investors. Encapsulating 20 years of experience analyzing funds, it shows you what works in fund investing. In addition to plain-English chapters on key topics, it includes real-world examples and 14 investor checklists. Hardbound, 6"x 9", 286 pages.

Answer Key

Lesson 301: Shades of Value

1   a. All value managers buy stocks that they believe are undervalued, but each manager defines value in a different way.

2   b. Relative-value managers measure a stock's value by comparing its price ratios with some benchmark.

3   a. Managers practicing absolute-value strategies calculate what a company is worth in absolute terms and will only buy the company's stock for less than that figure.

4   c. Styles can differ a lot within each camp. Absolute-value managers can calculate a company's worth in a variety of ways, while relative-value managers can compare a variety of price multiples against a variety of benchmarks.

5   a. Answer B might apply to relative-value managers who use a stock's industry as their benchmark. Answer C would apply to absolute-value managers who use a company's absolute worth as their benchmark.

Lesson 302: Shades of Growth

1   c. If a firm has announced bad news—lower-than-expected earnings, for example—its stock price is likely to fall in the short term. Momentum investors usually try to sell at that point. They tend to hold stocks that have posted strong earnings.

2   a. A value fund or a fund that buys stocks without earnings may buy Wal-Mart. But this solid, well-run company that generally meets or slightly exceeds quarterly earnings estimates would probably most appeal to a manager looking for steady growth.

3   c. GARP stands for growth at a reasonable price—a common investment strategy that looks for both growth and value qualities.

4   a. The blend column of the Morningstar style box is commonly home to funds that seek earnings growth at cheap prices.

5   b. Because momentum managers engage in frequent stock trading, momentum funds usually have high annual turnover rates. This trading and turnover is bad for tax efficiency. Momentum-type stocks also generally carry a lot of price risk (i.e., they're often expensive).

Lesson 303: Using Focused Funds

1 b. A focused fund owns a few stocks, invests a lot of its assets in its top-10 stocks, or both. One that has a manager's devoted attention is not necessarily a focused fund.
2 c. Owning a focused fund is most similar to owning a bunch of individual companies. Index funds tend to be broadly diversified reflections of a major market index. Fixed-income funds invest in bonds.
3 a. While a focused fund may have an inexperienced manager or high expenses, investors should almost always expect some short-term volatility.
4 c. Established and well-respected fund families are most likely to step in if a fund is dramatically underperforming its peer group, at least partially to protect its good name.
5 c. A focused fund with expenses higher than 2% should be regarded with suspicion.

Lesson 304: Style-Box-Specific vs. Flexible Funds

1 b. Managers who like to stay put stick to one area of the Morningstar style box. Families such as Putnam and T. Rowe Price use this approach.
2 c. Flexible managers aren't any better or worse than style-box purists. They're just different.
3 b. An all style-box-specific portfolio may not be the best portfolio, but it is easiest to build and maintain.
4 a. It is best to hold flexible funds outside your portfolio's core and monitor them rigorously.
5 c. Just as using flexible funds is a personal decision, so too is determining what to do if and when your flexible funds start to buy the same types of stocks.

Lesson 305: Sector-Fund Investing

1 a. You can build a very diverse portfolio without ever buying a sector fund.
       But you can use sector funds to diversify or to speculate.

2 b. Investors tend to buy sector funds as their performance is peaking.
       As a result, the average sector-fund investor doesn't do very well. Instead,
       favor less-popular sectors or add sector funds to diversify what you
       already have.

3 c. Redemption fees discourage short-term traders from buying a sector fund
       and are paid back into the fund—in other words, they are paid back
       to investors who remain in the fund. And if you are a long-term investor,
       you'll never have to pay these fees.

4 a. A fund investing only in Internet stocks is bound to be the most volatile.
       The more narrow the industry that the fund focuses on, the riskier it's
       bound to be.

5 a. To play a long-term theme, you need to be a long-term investor. If you
       believe in the idea, you should be buying when returns are down,
       or investing a little bit at a time (dollar-cost averaging) regardless of
       whether the fund's performance is up or down.

Lesson 306: Using Quirky Bond Funds

1 a. High-quality bond funds generally have a lot of interest-rate risk while
       high-yield and prime-rate funds do not. They have credit risk instead.

2 c. Inflation-indexed bonds are designed specifically to do well if inflation
       rises. Inflation has an eroding effect on the value of all other types
       of bonds.

3 c. Inflation-indexed bond funds generally stick with TIPS, which are issued
       by the U.S. Treasury. You can't get any higher quality than that!
       High-yield bond and prime-rate funds, meanwhile, hold securities from
       less-than-creditworthy companies.

4 b. High-yield bond funds own actual bonds from lower-quality companies,
       while inflation-indexed bond funds own bonds issued by the U.S.
       Treasury. Prime-rate funds own bank loans.

5 c. The bonds these funds own pay high yields because there is risk that
       the companies backing them won't be able to meet their obligations. Such
       defaults are most likely to crop up in a tougher economic environment.

Lesson 307: Bear-Proofing Your Portfolio

1   a. Investments lose money during a bear market. Not all bear markets are marked by rising inflation or recession.
2   c. Stocks of companies that produce must-have products, such as drugs or food, tend to do best during recessions. Those investments dependent upon a healthy economy, including junk bonds and cyclical stocks, tend to do poorly.
3   a. Hard assets, including gold and real estate, do best. Everything else gets ravaged.
4   b. Bonds tend to hold up relatively well in this environment. Because their dividends are effectively worth more in this type of economy, they have more purchasing power.
5   c. Building a diverse portfolio that owns a little bit of everything is the best way to bear-proof a portfolio. Timing the market by moving to cash rarely succeeds, while bear-market funds will lose money during a bull market.

Lesson 308: The Plight of the Fickle Investor

1   a. Fickle investors buy what's hot and sell what's not. Dollar-cost-averaging investors invest a little at a time.
2   c. Investors suffer most with aggressive funds, in which volatility and temptation are highest.
3   a. Investing a little at a time by setting up a regular dollar-cost-averaging program will prevent you from becoming a fickle investor.
4   b. Discipline pays with aggressive funds, so unless you can guarantee that you won't give in to the temptation to sell when the fund stalls, we would say ease into it by dollar-cost averaging. And we are not advocates of market-timing.
5   c. By expecting past results to carry on in the future, you are setting yourself up to become a fickle investor.

Lesson 309: Chasing Closed Funds

1 b. When funds close, returns often slow and tax efficiency worsens. Inflows, which are negligible once a fund closes, reduce the tax burden on all shareholders because there are more people to distribute capital gains to.
2 b. Funds usually close when inflows turn into torrents—and that usually happens when funds are undergoing a period of extraordinary performance. Performance often goes back to average (or worse).
3 a. Closings also make sense for funds with a small number of managers and analysts, or those that focus on less liquid asset classes such as small caps or REITs.
4 a. Funds that close at preset targets tend to continue to perform well after their closings.
5 b. Reopening is often a sign that an asset class is being overlooked.

Lesson 310: Buying the Unloved

1 a. Because fund investors often buy high and sell low (rather than the other way around), opportunists can make money by buying what others are selling.
2 b. We use cash flows to determine a category's popularity. Unpopular categories are often poor-performing categories, but not always.
3 b. Be sure to buy one fund from each category because not all unpopular categories thrive, nor do they thrive at the same time. Also, we recommend that you buy before June.
4 a. You should put no more than 5% of your assets into unpopular categories. This strategy is speculative. Yes, it has worked more often than not, but it's not meant to be a core part of your portfolio.
5 c. Popular categories tend to underperform unpopular categories. As such, think about taking some profits away from popular categories, but don't do wholesale selling. That practice may upset your asset allocation and lead to taxable events.

Lesson 311: Buying Rookie Funds

1 b. Steer clear of rookie fund managers who are rookies themselves. However, you might think about taking a chance with a rookie manager if he or she works at a fund family with a very clear style.

2 c. Without past return and risk statistics to guide your decision, the portfolio is the best indication of a fund's potential.

3 a. Managers who also own the funds they run are shareholders, too, which means they're more likely to keep costs lower and minimize taxable distributions.

4 b. As funds grow, they begin to enjoy economies of scale; in other words, there are more shareholders to cover costs.

5 b. We suggest you start out with a small position in a rookie fund, and if the fund lives up to your expectations, you can always add to it over time.

Lesson 312: Avoiding Portfolio Overlap

1 b. Investors are often surprised to find that their mutual funds own many of the same stocks they own. That means overlap.

2 a. If you own a lot of value funds, you're likely overweight in financial stocks. Growth managers may like telecom names, but they generally love tech stocks more than anything else.

3 c. Because the large-cap universe is small, there's little need to own a large-blend fund if you already have funds from the large-value and large-growth categories.

4 a. Managers generally have ingrained investment habits that they apply to every pool of money they run; they'll rarely use a growth strategy on one portfolio and a value strategy on another.

5 a. If you own more than one fund run by a boutique or specialist shop, chances are you own two (or more) of the same thing. Boutiques focus on what they do best, and as a result, owning more than one of their funds often results in overlap.

Lesson 313: Fund Warning Signs

1 b. As assets grow, expenses may decline. But performance may stall, and the fund's manager may have to change his or her strategy to accommodate all that money.

2 a. To accommodate asset growth, some fund managers will buy more stocks, buy larger companies, or trade less.

3 b. Manager changes can lead to a drop-off in performance or a change in strategy, so they're certainly warning signs. However, some types of funds handle manager changes better than others. As a result, a manager change isn't an automatic sell signal.

4 c. Changes at fund families can mean changes at your fund if your manager takes on new responsibilities or is otherwise distracted from running the fund that you own.

5 a. Fund performance isn't everything; it won't reflect a manager change, for example, or clue you in to changes that may be on the horizon.

Lesson 314: Where and Why Asset Size Matters

1 a. Small-cap stocks take up less than 10% of the U.S. market's overall assets; large caps, meanwhile, account for more than 80% of the market. It's therefore easier for a fund manager with a lot of assets to buy bigger companies than to own a small fry.

2 c. Value funds trade less than growth funds, and therefore they incur lower trading costs. The less trading, the lower the costs—and the easier it is to handle more assets.

3 a. Growth managers usually trade more than value managers, and they're competing with lots of other buyers for high-priced, high-growth stocks. Value managers, meanwhile, face a lot less competition because they favor securities that fewer investors want.

4 c. Funds can close or change their strategies when faced with too many assets, or the fund managers may hold cash or buy more stocks.

5 a. The less a fund trades, the lower its trading cost. Aggressive fast-trading funds will only be hurt more by asset growth. And by avoiding all growth funds, you're missing out on a large part of the market.

Lesson 315: When to Sell a Fund

1 c. If a fund loses or gains more than it should, it may be taking on risks that you didn't think it took. It may therefore be an inappropriate investment for you.

2 b. Funds can change styles without a strategy change. A manager may buy small-cap stocks, for example, but hold onto them as they grow into large-cap names. Thus, a small-cap fund may shift into a mid-cap fund without a full-blown strategy change.

3 c. Give funds a few years before cutting them loose, and be sure to compare them with appropriate benchmarks.

4 a. If your goals change, your portfolio should, too. Since you're now planning for a shorter-term goal, you may need to sell some of your aggressive funds and become more conservative.

5 c. While buying on dips or holding on to break even are strategies that many investors employ, you don't have to, as long as you know that you'd never make such a volatile investment again. Learn from your mistakes.

Lesson 316: Rebalancing Your Portfolio

1 a. Once you've built your portfolio, you need to monitor it and occasionally rebalance. If you leave your portfolio untouched, your allocations will change and no longer reflect your original goals and risk tolerance.

2 c. Investors who rebalance their investments at 18-month intervals reap many of the same benefits as those who rebalance more often. Moreover, these investors save themselves unnecessary labor and, in the case of taxable investments, some money.

3 c. Morningstar studies have found that investors obtain the most risk control from rebalancing by asset class.

4 a. When it comes to subasset classes or investment styles, rebalance by the numbers, not the calendar.

5 b. Rebalancing means adding money to poor performers that are taking up less and less of your portfolio.

Lesson 317: Calculating Your Personal Rate of Return

1 c. Reported returns are based on lump-sum investments over specific time periods. If you use dollar-cost averaging or if you invest in a fund at any other time than at the start of the period, your personal returns will differ from the reported ones.

2 c. Knowing your portfolio's actual returns can help you determine whether you're on track to meet your investment goals and whether your funds are living up to your expectations.

3 c. Fund companies rarely include personal rates of return on documents. You'll have to calculate the number for yourself by using a financial calculator or spreadsheet program, or by entering your portfolio in Portfolio Manager on Morningstar.com.

4 b. The returns you're calculating are for the final worth of your portfolio, minus the money you started with and invested during the year.

5 c. Just because your personal rate of return is lower than a reported rate of return over a given time period doesn't mean that you won't meet your goals. It may, however, mean that you're making trades at inopportune times, thereby sabotaging your results.

Lesson 318: Calculating Your Cost Basis

1 b. You use cost basis, the price you paid for a security, to determine your profit or loss when you sell shares.

2 a. To determine your profit or loss, subtract the cost basis from the current selling price. The difference is the amount the government taxes.

3 c. While FIFO—first in, first out—is the most basic method, other methods can save you more money in certain situations, depending on your purchase prices, how long you've held the shares, and the current share price.

4 b. If you sell the first shares you bought, you're using FIFO. If you ask the fund to sell shares you paid the most for but have held for at least one year, you're using the specific-shares method.

5 a. In this method, shares are divided into short-term and long-term gains and are then averaged for cost basis. If you have no short-term gains, you're basically using the single-category averaging method—you have only long-term gains.

Lesson 319: Is Your Retirement Portfolio on Track?

1 c. Social Security, pensions or employer-sponsored retirement plans, and personal savings should be components of your nest egg. Your own personal savings will likely make the difference between a retirement of jet-setting and one of sweater knitting.

2 c. You don't need to go through this exercise each time you take a look at or rebalance your portfolio, but it's a good idea to run through the numbers every few years so that you're not caught by surprise when retirement comes.

3 b. Though stocks returned 18% per year, on average, during the 1990s, we recommend a more conservative number.

4 b. Intermediate-term bonds have returned 5.3% per year, on average, since 1926, according to Ibbotson Associates.

5 a. You should get more aggressive only if your retirement is far enough away—say, 10 or more years off. Otherwise, you may be taking too much risk.

Lesson 320: Refining Your Portfolio

1 b. Not every life event has to trigger changes for every investors' portfolio. But we should all re-evaluate our financial plans as we pass through a life stage.

2 a. The first step is deciding what you want. Are you looking for someone to handle part of your financial life or are you seeking a financial advisor who can take care of it all? Talk to advisors and gather references after you know what you need.

3 c. The ADV form includes advisors' educational backgrounds and professional designations. It also discusses how the advisor is compensated, and whether he or she has ties to particular insurance or mutual fund companies.

4 a. Compare a company's sales growth with those of other companies
        in the same sector. Examine whether sales growth is speeding
        up or slowing down, as well as how consistent growth has been.
5 c. Return on assets, or ROA, is a key measure of how well a company
        uses investors' money.

Also in the Morningstar
Fearless Investing Series

Find the Right Mutual Funds

Our beginning-level workbook shows you how to find mutual funds best meeting your investing objectives.

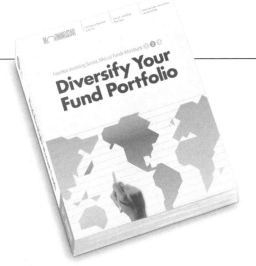

Diversify Your Fund Portfolio

Our intermediate-level workbook explains and illustrates how to build a profitable portfolio of mutual funds.

Coming in Summer 2005—Morningstar Fearless Investing Series for Stocks